THE INVISIBLE HANDS OF U.S. COMMERCIAL BANKING REFORM

The Invisible Hands of U.S. Commercial Banking Reform

Private Action and Public Guarantees

by

Margaret M. Polski
Institute for Development Strategies,
Indiana University, Bloomington, U.S.A.

KLUWER ACADEMIC PUBLISHERS
BOSTON / DORDRECHT / LONDON

A C.I.P. Catalogue record for this book is available from the Library of Congress.

ISBN 1-4020-7462-X

Published by Kluwer Academic Publishers,
P.O. Box 17, 3300 AA Dordrecht, The Netherlands.

Sold and distributed in North, Central and South America
by Kluwer Academic Publishers,
101 Philip Drive, Norwell, MA 02061, U.S.A.

In all other countries, sold and distributed
by Kluwer Academic Publishers,
P.O. Box 322, 3300 AH Dordrecht, The Netherlands.

Printed on acid-free paper

Printed in the Netherlands.

Table of Contents

Dedication

In memory of my parents, Philip and Catherine Polski, who taught me to keep my eye on the ball, and for Lin and Vincent Ostrom, who gave me a court in which to play.

Preface

This book is a product of my commitment to developing both theory and practice in political economy. I first became interested in economic and institutional change in the commercial banking industry when I took a seminar on financial institutions led by Robert Glauber in the Kennedy School of Government at Harvard University in the spring of 1995. In my experience, Bob is one of a handful of teachers who has the verve to challenge and inspire both esoteric and practical inquiry: the seminar grappled with practical business and policy problems in a way that posed a significant challenge to existing theories. In addition to demonstrating the need to better integrate theory and practice, it provided a perspective and an approach that I continue to find useful in research, consulting, and teaching.

Conducting the research for this study has taught me many things about banking, regulation, and policy making, and I am grateful to a very large number of people for their assistance. Bob Glauber continues to be generous in discussing the challenges of change in the financial services industry. Colleagues in the Workshop in Political Theory and Policy Analysis and the Institute for Development Strategies at Indiana University as well as a workshop on the future of banking in the advanced economies held in March, 2002 at the European University Institute have also been enormously helpful: David Audretsch, Richard Deeg, Marcello di Cecco, Jeff Hart, Michele Fratianni, Lin and Vincent Ostrom, Daniel Verdier, and Elmus Wicker have been particularly generous. I owe a particular debt to Thráinn Eggertsson, who provided encouragement at one of those critical points that are the bane of an author's existence. Last but not least, I am deeply indebted to clients and other executives and professionals in the financial services industry, policy makers, and friends and colleagues too numerous to mention who have discussed issues and events with me, shared their experience and perspective, read chapters, tolerated my single-mindedness, and enthusiastically encouraged me to press on. Naturally, none of these generous people bear any responsibility for the product of this study – all errors and omissions are mine alone.

Margaret Polski
November 2002

CHAPTER ONE

Introduction

This is a book about real life and big ideas. The real life is economic and institutional change in the U.S. commercial banking industry. Over the period 1975 to 2000, the regulatory barriers that strictly separated banking, insurance, and securities market activities eroded. Substantially all banking assets are now controlled by holding companies that own a broad range of financial services enterprises, prohibitions against interstate banking have fallen, and financial holding companies are now permitted to engage in a more diversified set of activities including securities underwriting, investment management, mutual funds, insurance, municipal finance, and corporate investment banking. In addition, banks have implemented a number of process innovations that change the nature of banking.

Coincident with corporate and regulatory restructuring activities, the banking industry has consolidated. While the U.S. banking industry is far more diverse and fragmented than that of any other advanced economy, it is considerably more homogeneous and concentrated today than it was for most of the 20th century. The number of commercial banks declined from 14,384 in 1975 to 8,315 as of December 31, 2000. At the end of 2001, the twenty-five largest banking organizations held 62% of industry assets. And most banking experts believe consolidation will continue in coming years.

While these changes represent the completion of a critical stage in restructuring and modernizing the U.S. financial system, to some observers, the process was mind-bogglingly complex and unredeemably wasteful. Moreover, as revelations of conflicts of interest and ill-considered management decisions in the financial services industry are revealed, some policymakers are questioning the wisdom of deregulation and proposing new restraints. This is where the big ideas come in. We have no theory that fully explains economic and institutional change in banking or that allows us to assess and compare the governance of the U.S. banking system with governance of other regulatory systems.[1] Standard theory assumes that a social mechanism

[1] For an analysis of the political and structural implications of different types of credit allocation systems, see Zysman (1983). For a macro-level analysis of state-societal relations in the context of business competition, see Hart (1992). For a more recent argument that financial systems function as a type of industrial policy by shaping access to and the cost of business finance and hence the competitive advantage of a country, see Mowery (1992). For an overview of work in comparative financial systems, see Allen and Gale (2001).

exists that either functions like a neutral social planner that seamlessly reconciles diverse interests to produce socially optimal outcomes or functions at the service of a self-interested group of rent-seekers who are unconstrained in their ability to allocate resources to serve their own short-term advantage. While recent literature on financial regulation and deregulation has provided some useful insights, significant gaps remain.

Regulatory change in the U.S. financial system is connected to the broader question of governance under different constitutional designs. This question has been fodder for lively debate in the U.S. since the Federalists first defended the implications of the proposed constitution. Madison argued that the system of governance that could best achieve liberty and prosperity for all members of the newly independent states would make reform difficult; ". . . supplying by opposite and rival interest, the defect of better motives" (Madison, 1788, in Cooke, 1961). One hundred years later, in the throes of industrialization and with Americans embracing bureaucratic organization based on principles of scientific management, Woodrow Wilson took issue with this conception, arguing that in reality, the U.S. system of government has an acknowledged center of power that serves the interests of society by making reform less difficult, that ". . . those checks and balances have proved mischievous just to the extent to which they have succeeded in establishing themselves as realities," (Wilson [1887 (1956)]).

In the late 20th century, in the midst of widespread domestic and global political-economic restructuring, scholars reflecting on reformability and good governance placed a foot in each camp – the polycentric institutional design defended by the Federalists, and the more monocentric design Wilson promoted. They found value in both approaches, depending upon the policy context. For example, Lindblom (1979) argued that decentralized, pluralist decision-making is superior to centralized coordination for "ordinary issues," those issues necessarily involving a broad range of participants and interests and for which the connection between policy, reason, and values is obscure. However, "grand issues," in his view, lend themselves to more centralized approaches. In a similar vein, Wildavsky (1987) argued that institutional arrangements should join decentralized competition with more centralized planning.

But rather than answering questions about the nature of economic and institutional change, these debates merely beg classic questions of political economy and policy analysis: under a given set of conditions, what is the role of government in creating incentives for political and economic activity and what is the path to change? Banking reform provides an opportunity to closely analyze a number of interesting questions related to economic and institutional change in one of the most elaborate forms of polycentric governance that has emerged from the U.S. constitutional design. Coordination and collective action in this type of system are not addressed in the existing literatures on regulation and political economy. Both the empirical realities and the theoretical logic of the dynamics of polycentric systems are, at present, open questions.

This study makes a small start in this direction by examining the causes and process of U.S. commercial banking reform. Using a case study approach, the investigation addresses the following questions about banking reform:

1. What stimulated change? When reform efforts emerged, were they in response to a failure or to an opportunity? What was the source of the opportunity or failure – markets, governments, institutions, or something else?
2. What was the process of change, e.g. what types of economic and institutional changes occurred and how were they associated? What was the role of competition? Who was involved, what were their motivations for making change, and which processes did they use?
3. Finally, what lessons can be drawn from recent experience that can be applied to future reform efforts?

Approach

There are few analyses of regulatory reform that explicitly develop the linkage between institutions and economic performance. General theories of change do not provide the kind of micro foundations that are necessary to compare one reform situation to another or one institutional design to another. Nor do theories provide guidance for policy makers who confront the practical challenge of developing effective strategies for institutional change. By micro foundations I mean a fairly precise specification of a policy choice environment including the principal policy makers and their roles, information, and resources, the possible outcomes in a given policy choice situation and the payoffs associated with these outcomes, and the strategies that policy makers can employ to achieve these outcomes.

Banking reform is a good example of a naturally occurring field experiment in very large scale, polycentric collective choice. However, investigating decision-making in a polycentric system poses a substantial scientific challenge. A field experiment is rife with violations of internal and external validity, which confound formal analysis. To further complicate the analysis, other studies of economic and institutional change suggest that the process involves path-dependent, dynamic choice by individuals who are boundedly rational.[2] While one can abstract from reality in order to create simple models that are amenable to formal methods of study, one does so at the risk of losing important detail. Absent sufficient knowledge of a particular political-economic situation, abstraction is premature and leads to very poor policy advice. More generally, theories of regulation and institutional political economy are in their infancy. Knowledge about choice behavior in polycentric systems is scant. Hence, it is difficult to justify simplifications that are not based upon intensive study of real settings: one of the challenges this study addresses is

[2] See for example the extensive work of Douglass North on economic and institutional change in western societies.

systematically analyzing economic and institutional change in a polycentric decision environment.

Most scholars agree that advances in the theory and practice of political economy require comparative institutional analysis. Comparison is enhanced by placing theories of events and outcomes in the context of a detailed description of the institutional environment in which actors make institutional choices and the conditions under which they must act. Once this has been accomplished for a particular class of decision environments and there is a sufficiently large body of data, it is then possible to analyze these data using more formal methods. One could, for example, extract principles from a particular study (or better still, cumulate studies using the same methods), and specify a decision environment that could then be studied using experimental methods in an artificial environment or in the laboratory.

While banking reform is a one-shot case in the universe of all regulatory reforms, an analysis of this reform involves examining the behavior of many actors over multiple years in a large, heterogeneous political-economic system. It thus requires grappling with millions of discrete observations on multiple variables. Narrowing and focusing this kind of investigation requires multiple methods and a heavily structured approach. The approach taken in this study incorporates historical, qualitative, and quantitative analyses. Analysis proceeds from theoretically relevant questions. Whenever possible, inferences are drawn based upon quantitative analysis of data drawn from public records, industry reports, and empirical studies compiled by banking regulators and other reliable banking experts. Quantitative analyses are illustrated graphically and backed up by tables of raw data.

A number of different frameworks are used to organize the analysis. The use of frameworks makes the process of investigating change more transparent and improves the reliability of the analysis. The analytical logic of the Institutional Analysis and Development (IAD) framework provides a superstructure for the entire study.[3] A second framework, which integrates arguments in the literature on economic growth, is used more transparently to guide the analysis of the economic and institutional dynamics of the reform process.[4] Edward Mason's Structure-Conduct-Performance paradigm provides a general guide for analyzing patterns of interaction and outcomes.[5]

The heart of the study is an analysis of statistics on banking reform over the period 1960–2000. Intensive regulation of the commercial banking industry has generated data about banking activities that have been collected systematically over a long

---

[3] The IAD framework, which was developed by scholars in the Workshop in Political Theory and Policy Analysis at Indiana University, focuses analysis on behavior in a policy situation or "action arena," which includes the action situation and individuals and groups who are routinely involved in the situation. One aspect of the analysis is to identify physical and material conditions, community attributes, and rules that affect behavior in the policy situation. Two other aspects of the analysis involve identifying and evaluating patterns of interactions and outcomes. For an overview of the IAD framework and its application to policy analysis and design, see Polski and E. Ostrom (1999).

[4] See Chapter Three.

[5] For a description of Mason's paradigm, see Scherer and Ross (1990).

period of time by federal and state regulators, industry specialists, academics, and consumer advocacy groups.[6] The period 1960–1970 represents a base period, which precedes the first liberalization of interstate banking legislation. The 1960s are generally viewed as a stable and relatively mature period in U.S. banking history when banks faced little competition, so they are a good starting point for the analysis. The period 1970–2000 represents the change period. The empirical analysis makes it possible to speculate about incentives for economic and institutional change, extrapolate lessons about the fundamental principles of polycentric governance, and identify areas for further research.

Overview

Banking regulation has been the subject of great controversy and considerable policy experimentation in the United States since the colonial era. Inextricably linked to the growth and development of both regional economies and government institutions, the organization and regulation of banking was a subject of conflict between England and the New England colonies as well as one of the first policy contests waged in the spirit of the new republic's constitutionally mandated choice mechanism of "opposite and rival interests." The modern structure of U.S. commercial banking, which has evolved into a quasi-public form that combines voluntary and involuntary coordination mechanisms, is the product of policy experiments that have run the full gamut from government to market control.

The origins of more recent policy experiments can be traced back to the 1960s, when non-financial companies formed Banking Holding Companies (BHCs) in order to acquire banks and banks began reorganizing under BHC umbrellas in order to diversify their financial activities. This development prompted the Board of Governors of the Federal Reserve to ask the U.S. Congress to amend the Banking Holding Company Act to tighten its ability to regulate BHCs. Congress complied, passing the Douglas Amendments in 1970. However, the terms of the debate changed in the late 1970s when state governments began liberalizing restrictions on diversification and the U.S. Congress began holding hearings on financial modernization. The state of Maine launched the first salvo in 1975 when it passed legislation that permitted banks headquartered in other states to branch into the state through bank holding companies, providing that the branching BHC's home state offered reciprocal privileges to BHC's incorporated in Maine. By 1979, when Maine's legislation took effect, the U.S. Congress had commenced hearings on structural change in the financial services industry.

Over the period 1970 to 2000, U.S. commercial banks reorganized, consolidated, and implemented a number of process innovations, regulators eased restrictions on bank activities and executed more than 1,504 closure or assistance

[6] Data sources include statistics and reports published by the Board of Governors of the Federal Reserve, the Federal Deposit Insurance Corporation (FDIC), U.S. Department of Commerce, the U.S. Congress, and the U.S. Department of the Treasury.

transactions involving more than $230 billion in assets, all fifty states liberalized restrictions on bank activities, and the U.S. Congress enacted fifteen statutory changes. These reforms were focused on leveling the playing field among banks and other firms engaged in financial services activities, allowing bank holding companies to diversify into activities beyond traditional banking products and services, and giving markets a greater role in regulating banks than governments.

The assumption that drove public debate about banking reform in the late 20th century was that the chief source of failure in the banking industry was government regulation: the prescribed antidote was more market regulation and less government regulation. Modern proponents of banking reform argued that reforms were required to create economic incentives that would improve the safety and soundness of the banking system. Arguments for reform reflected two policy design principles, which spring from standard economic theories about regulating private goods: (1) promote efficiency by encouraging competition between financial intermediaries and permitting consolidation to reduce excess supply, and (2) promote innovation by permitting diversification. The political debate focused on diversification, where reform required action in both the private and public sectors to reorganize, loosen regulatory requirements, and liberalize state and federal banking laws.

A prominent justification for liberalization among academics and other banking experts was that geographic and product restrictions increased the risk of bank failures and panics by inhibiting diversification against local economic downturns.[7] Evidence was presented that banks that were operating in markets protected from interstate competition charged higher loan rates, paid lower deposit rates, and provided fewer customer services than those banks that were subject to interstate competition. It was further argued that the appropriate geographic market for banking services depends critically upon the nature of the service, e.g., corporate and private banking services exist in national and international markets, whereas individual and small business services tend to be local. In response to critics who argued that diversification would encourage destabilizing predatory behavior within the industry, contradictory evidence was presented for states that had eased restrictions such as California and New York.

Those who sought to preserve prohibitions against diversification were also worried about bank failures and panics. However, they argued that allowing banks to diversify would lead to widespread consolidation in bank ownership, which would increase the market power of banks while decimating the supervisory checks and balances of the existing banking system. Theoretical and empirical arguments were made that given the inherent moral hazard and adverse selection problems in the U.S. banking system and the difficulty of perfectly supervising bank behavior, consolidation would increase the number of banks that were "too big to fail" and result in a national banking crisis of devastating proportions.

Opponents had other concerns as well. Subject to recessionary pressures as a function of structural change in the economy, states were increasingly concerned

---

[7] See White (1986) for a summary of studies and citations.

about their ability to compete for investment capital for economic development and to finance local government activities. Maintaining local control of financial resources was a politically popular strategy to facilitate capital accumulation at state and regional levels. Many state governments were afraid that nationwide banking would lead to local capital flight, e.g., that the deposits of local investors would not be invested in local economic development but in developing the economy of another (competing) state.

Bank owners and managers in small communities in the U.S., whose interests were represented by the Independent Bankers' Association, wanted to maintain the quiet life afforded by their highly protected markets. Some were afraid that diversified banking would lead to hostile merger and acquisition activity, interfering with their ability to maintain their favored position in the community, keep their jobs, or to sell their banks on the most favorable terms. Consumer groups were concerned that banks owned out-of-state would not serve community needs as well as banks owned in-state. Finally, state banking authorities persistently argued that federal action to permit diversification would violate states' rights.

Last, but by no means least, members of the insurance and securities industries were concerned that diversified banking would position banks to destroy their markets. Banks already owned a very large but fragmented national retail distribution network. Interstate banking and branching would link this network. If Congress then allowed banks to enter insurance and securities markets, some argued that banks could handily dominate financial services.

As frequently occurred in the first 100 years of banking, in the late twentieth century, the U.S. banking industry was deeply troubled and existing institutional arrangements were failing to provide the coordination required to revitalize the industry. There were plausible arguments on both sides of the diversification issue but little conclusive evidence regarding the probable effects of change, considerable domestic and international economic uncertainty, and an established history of control by the states rather than federal government. Moreover, the structure of governance under the U.S. Constitution requires that the policy making process incorporate numerous inputs and choice mechanisms, hence policy change is more evolutionary than revolutionary. And so despite a strongly committed core of reformers in both the public and private sectors who worked on committees and task forces, testified, lobbied, and repeatedly sponsored and cosponsored initiatives, legislation repealing restrictions on diversification was not passed at the federal level until the 1990s. Yet when the Riegle Neal Act was passed in 1994, which permitted interstate banking through banking holding companies, nationwide banking had already been legally implemented. And when the Graham, Leach, Bliley Act was passed in 2000, which repealed restrictions on banks' activities in securities and insurance that had been imposed under the Glass Steagall Act, bank holding companies were already legally engaged in these activities.

No existing theory of regulation or economic and institutional change predicts that U.S. commercial banking would reform as it has. This is in large part because the existing literature on commercial banking regulation tends to focus on how banks *should* be regulated rather than how banks *are* regulated and the behavior that logically follows from a particular governance regime. Hence, studying the process of economic and institutional change provides the opportunity to examine standard assumptions about regulation and formulate new theories of change. Chapter Two provides a broad survey of the literature on regulation and U.S. banking reform. Three perspectives on economic and institutional change emerge from this survey:

(1) The Social Welfare perspective, which assumes that change occurs in response to a market failure, that the motivation for change is to achieve efficiency, and that the process of change is rational and seamlessly orchestrated by a mechanism that functions like a neutral social planner who is able to enforce efficient allocation of economic surplus;
(2) The Distributional perspective, which assumes that change is stimulated by government failure, that the motivation for change is to obtain economic rents and votes, and that the process of change is rational and orchestrated through the legislative process in response to interest group pressure;
(3) The Institutional perspective, which assumes that failure stems from the rules of the game, that the motivation for change is to economize on transaction costs, and that the process of change is a boundedly rational search for alternative rules that is itself constrained by the governance process within which it is embedded.

Regardless of their perspective on political economy, the explanations of other scholars are incomplete: we simply do not understand as much as we could about the nature of banking regulation in the United States and the causes and processes of change. Moreover, our assumptions are leading us away from developing a better understanding of the forces that operate in the U.S. political economy. Chapter Three addresses this problem by linking the banking regulation literature to what we know about the fundamental sources of economic and institutional change. Integrating theories and evidence on economic and institutional change suggests that holding all other situational factors constant, change is a dynamic, adaptive response to shocks in the economic and institutional environment (Δ) that is a function of changes in beliefs about competitiveness (B), changes in governance (G), which interact with the institutional environment in which they are embedded to create incentives for individual and collective action, and changes in economizing (E), which interact with the economic environment and represent a particular configuration of economic factors and production processes:

$$\Delta = F\ (B, G, E)$$

The ability to respond adaptively to changes in the economic and institutional environment depends critically upon the types of individuals who are present in the situation – their personality structures and norms, their ability to generate and select from an array of alternatives and then effectively implement change, regulation and other rules of the game, and economic resources.

Testing this model of change requires investigating different types of change: competitive shocks, which occur in the industry and larger economic and institutional environments in which the industry operates, changes in beliefs, which begin with individuals who make decisions and engage in collective action in the private and public sectors, changes in governance, which involve transacting between individuals and firms as well as regulating the activities of firms, and changes in economizing, which are located in production and distribution processes. Empirical support requires demonstrating that:

1. There is a change in the economic or institutional environment that creates new opportunities or threatens the status quo;
2. Changes in the economic and institutional environment affect beliefs about the competitive situation;
3. Coincident with changes in opportunities or threats and beliefs, there are observable changes in governance;
4. Coincident with changes in opportunities or threats and beliefs, there are observable changes in economizing.

Chapter Four begins by describing the nature of commercial banking. From a systemic perspective, modern banking functions more like a club good than a private good: because banking is based upon a fractional reserve system, banks create money when they lend, hence consumption is neither strictly rivalrous nor perfectly excludable. Mass consumption of banking services exhibits both positive and negative externalities, which means that without effective coordinating institutions, the activities of individual banks can produce inflation and frequent financial crises.

After reviewing some of the specific features of commercial banking in the U.S., data are introduced that demonstrate how changes in the relative prices of money and information processing, two key inputs into the economics of banking, altered the competitive environment of banking and changed beliefs about what was required to effectively compete in financial services. An analysis of trends in aggregate data for the whole commercial banking industry over the period 1960–2000, shows that significant changes in structure, conduct, and performance are associated with changes in the economic and institutional environment and beliefs about rivalry.

Chapter Five begins by examining the institutional structure and political economy of banking regulation from colonial times through contemporary reform. The current system for regulating banking is a hybrid compromise between a government controlled credit allocation system and a market-based credit allocation system. This design evolved to accommodate the remarkably stable American preference for locally controlled credit allocation and the need to coordinate across a very large and diverse economy to protect the safety and soundness of the system. While U.S. banking regulation is quite complex, once understood in political-economic context, the design has an internal elegance that is deeply rooted in constitutional design, collective action traditions, and the exigencies of economic integration in a large and very fragmented political economy.

Analysis of aggregate institutional change in the U.S. commercial banking industry over the period 1960–2000, indicates that very significant changes in governance are associated with changes in the economic and institutional environment and beliefs about competition. Bank managers led the process, relying on three governance strategies to compete more effectively and side-step regulatory constraints on diversification: they reorganized as bank holding companies, merged with other banks and acquired other types of financial services enterprises, and implemented process innovations. Regulators and legislators also played key roles in institutional change. Regulators encouraged competition by granting large numbers of new bank charters, acquiesced to the industry's demand to diversify by liberally interpreting rules that allowed bank holding companies to engage in activities closely related to banking, and encouraged consolidation by approving mergers and acquisitions that appeared to strengthen the capital structure of the industry. In a closely related but incremental series of actions, legislators at state and federal levels gradually removed restraints on powers, some of which had existed for over 200 years.

Reflecting upon the economic and institutional changes described in Chapters Four and Five, Chapter Six concludes the analysis by looking at evidence on economizing, speculates about incentives for change, and draws lessons for further research. In general, the data are consistent with three of the four assumptions about the causes and processes associated with economic and institutional change that are formulated in Chapter Three. However, the support for economizing is ambiguous. An analysis of changes in transaction costs in the commercial banking industry over the period 1960–2000, provides only partial support for the theory of transaction cost economizing. Over the long term, the evidence supports the assumption that firms seek to minimize transaction costs. However, over the short and medium term, transaction cost economizing does not appear to be associated with institutional change. A review of secondary sources suggests that consistent with this finding, there is limited evidence that banks have improved cost efficiency. Instead, it appears that banks have sought profit efficiency rather than strict cost efficiency, particularly those banks that have made mergers and acquisitions.

Incentives to pursue banking reform appear to emerge from the interdependencies created by a confluence of economic conditions, the governance structure of banking firms, the institutional structure of deposit guarantees, and the role of the banking industry in regional and national economic growth. Not all banks had incentives to support reform and many actively resisted the efforts of other members of the industry. However, as firms reorganized in order to compete in a changing economic environment, the governance structure they adopted created incentives to pursue reform through diversification. When competitive conditions created significant financial distress in the banking industry, the institutional structure of deposit guarantees created an incentive for regulators to partner with banks in implementing diversification strategies that would improve profits and build capital reserves. Similarly, the structure of finance for economic development in the U.S. created incentives for legislators to partner with regulators and banks to make reforms that would protect the economic vitality of the banking system.

Given the magnitude of change that has occurred in the U.S. commercial banking industry, it is entirely possible that more time must pass before we can accurately assess the nature of change. However, a number of lessons can be drawn from this study of the banking case. First, economic and institutional change in the U.S.

banking system is evolutionary rather than revolutionary, which suggests the need for more research on change from an evolutionary perspective. Moreover, it is clear that economic and institutional changes are closely linked: concerted efforts to systematically study these linkages are needed. Second, we could use a better understanding of motivation and change and in particular, the dynamics of competition. Banking has a tripartite regulatory structure that consists of private equity investors, private debt holders, and contingent public debt holders, yet there is no explicit research on how this kind of regime operates under different sets of conditions. And it is not at all clear how competitive forces operate – if at all – under this type of governance structure. Finally, there is much to be learned about the dynamics of polycentric systems, including the trade-offs associated with alternative coordination mechanisms.

An epilogue to this study speculates about the challenges facing bankers, regulators, and policy makers in the 21st century. After recovering smartly from the crises of the 1980s and early 1990s and generating nearly a decade of strong financial performance, banks are again showing signs of weakness. The legacy of economic and institutional change in the late 20th century may yet create pressure for cost efficiency while profits from traditional financial services are competed away. At the same time, new developments in life sciences and information technologies are placing new demands on financial systems. As the economies of the world continue to restructure, deepening levels of financial integration are creating systemic risks that banks and regulatory systems are ill-prepared to manage. How the industry copes with these challenges will depend upon how well the next generation of bank executives, regulators, and policy makers solve the problem of satisfying markets and governments by building and sustaining economic value without compromising systemic stability.

CHAPTER TWO

Theoretical Foundations

Economic and institutional change has challenged scholars and policy makers for centuries. Before there were social scientists seeking to engineer social change by writing policy prescriptions and testifying before legislative committees, there were philosophers who "whispered in the ears of princes." Whether they were justifying the perpetuation of an existing order, like Aristotle or Hayek, explaining conflict, like Thucydides or Karl Marx, or like Adam Smith or John Maynard Keynes, searching for principles upon which one might craft change in an existing order, they have all worked in the field of political economy.

The political economy literature is extensive, crossing not just centuries but disciplines, including philosophy, history, economics, political science, finance, and law. There are excellent surveys of this literature in these disciplines; hence the effort is not repeated here. Instead, what follows is an overview of the contemporary literature that is most relevant to explaining change in the U.S. commercial banking industry in the late twentieth century. As we shall see, these theories raise many questions. Moreover, as Peltzman (1989) and Stigler (1992) have observed, they fail to answer important questions about institutional flexibility.

1. Perspectives on Economic and Institutional Change

The central problem of modern political economy is to understand the role of government in economic affairs *vis à vis* markets. As Adam Smith (1776) speculated, powerful as it may be, the invisible hand of private interest operating in free markets can still fail to efficiently allocate economic surplus for certain types of goods and services.[1] When markets fail as allocation mechanisms, Smith argued

[1] Building on Smith's original insights, modern scholarship has produced a number of explanations for market failure: information is costly, it is not freely shared, or there is significant uncertainty; there are transaction costs; markets for some goods do not exist; there is market power either favoring producers (monopoly or oligopoly) or consumers (monopsony); there are production or consumption externalities (the positive or negative difference between price and true social cost); the nature of the good or service is inconsistent with a market governance mechanism, e.g. public goods and common-pool resources, and so on.

that it is the duty of government to coordinate by regulating private behavior. In Smith's view, regulation should be designed to configure private incentives so that self-interested individual behavior will, in the aggregate, produce economically efficient outcomes.

Commercial banking and other forms of intermediated commercial finance, such as insurance, are good examples of industries that arise as a function of market failure. Information deficits, uncertainty, and moral hazard make it difficult for individuals to evaluate and monitor certain types of financial risk, which inhibits their ability to trade directly in capital markets without intermediaries who have specialized knowledge and skill. In these types of financing situations, obligational markets with relational contracting can often better align information and incentives than markets. Moreover, intermediaries can achieve economies of scale that cannot be achieved in markets by aggregating the costs of transforming many diverse transactions that originate in small volumes. At the same time, centuries of experience have taught us that many types of financial activities – particularly banking – have externalities that require regulatory oversight.

The scholarly literature pertaining to regulation in the United States can be categorized based on the author's approach to political economy, which takes one of three forms; social welfare, distributional, or institutional.[2] The social welfare approach assumes that the main purpose of regulation is to promote the interest of society as a whole and that it is both possible and desirable to design policy and oversight activities that will re-engineer self interest to achieve economic efficiency. From this perspective, the source of failure is markets and the stimulus for change is economic inefficiency. The reform process is conceptualized as a constrained optimization problem in which a neutral, socially benign government intervenes to create information and incentives that redirect private actors away from socially inefficient behavior toward efficient behavior. Prominent contributions to this literature include Pigou (1932) who analyzes the problem of externalities, Musgrave's (1959) analysis of public economies, "public interest" theories of regulation, and work recognizing information constraints such as that of Stiglitz (1989) and Laffont and Tirole (1993).[3]

The distributional political economy approach to explaining regulatory change assumes that government fails to produce socially efficient outcomes. This approach focuses on the way in which governments and polities intervene to create and enforce legislation that allocates economic surplus. Distributional theorists argue that economic regulation is produced by policymakers who are subject to "capture" by

---

[2] Dixit (1996) and Peltzman (1989) have described the social welfare economics perspective as a "normative" approach to theory. Noll (1989a) and Vietor (1994) describe it as the "public interest" view. Peltzman (1989) has described distributional political economy theories as "economic." They are also sometimes referred to as "private-interest" theories. Finally, the "new institutional economics," is often cited as the home of theories that are ascribed here to institutional political economy.

[3] See Noll (1989a, 1989b), Joskow and Rose (1989), and Noll and Owen (1983) for summaries and discussion of the literature on public interest theories of regulation. Note that in recent years, Stiglitz has taken a strong interest in institutional approaches to political economy.

special interest groups, which seek economic rents.[4] Analysts working from this perspective assume that political interests are shaped by economic interests and then apply standard economic concepts about preferences and decision making, which may be subject to some form of informational constraint on rationality such as information and risk asymmetries, uncertainty, or time inconsistency. There are two interrelated strands of distributional political economy literature that pertain to regulatory change: one in economics, and the other in political science. Economic theories can be traced to Stigler's (1971) effort to build a general theory of the motivation for regulation. Political theories, which are broadly consistent with Fiorina's (1977) theory of distributive politics, emphasize governance failures and the process of institutional change.

Rather than assuming that individuals and groups behave consistently with standard economic assumptions about preferences and choice, institutionally oriented political economists focus on how an existing set of institutional arrangements shape the behavior of individuals and groups in responding to economic events. The governing "rules of the game" exist in multiple arenas in private and public sectors, including bi-lateral contracting, financial exchanges, organizations, legislative bodies, regulatory authorities, legal systems, and so on. Thus both markets and governments can fail to efficiently allocate economic surplus by devising and enforcing sub-optimal rules. While institutional theorists incorporate standard concepts from economics, they modify classical assumptions to take into consideration not only information constraints, but transaction costs arising from the structure of collective action and coordination mechanisms, property rights, or social norms for cooperation and trust. Preferences and decision-making processes are assumed to be boundedly rational rather than strictly rational. Prominent contributions to the institutional political economy perspective can be found in the work of Coase (1937, 1960), Williamson (1985, 1996), and North (1993). Table 2.1 compares the three perspectives.

---

[4] Following standard economic theory, economic rents are producer profits in excess of the point at which the marginal cost of production equals price. This surplus may or may not be associated with allocative inefficiency. That is, rents are not the same as monopoly profits. A firm can earn a rent from a productivity improvement that permits it to increase market share. It is a rent and not a monopoly profit if the firm cannot supply the entire market. In a competitive industry, rents are dissipated over the long-term as other firms match the first-mover's competitive advantage. Consumers can also reap rents if price is lower than the marginal cost of production, as can occur when there is excess production capacity in a market, e.g. supply exceeds demand. In a competitive market, supply will eventually equilibrate with demand and price will rise as financially stronger firms drive out weaker firms. Rents are frequently observed in the U.S. economy. Pursuit of rents is variously referred to as rent seeking, seeking competitive advantage, or "good business." Observing the potential for time-inconsistency problems inherent in capturing returns on innovation, Breyer (1982) argues that discouraging rent seeking may not be a desirable policy goal if it would constrain the search for efficiency (which would impede macroeconomic economic growth and development).

Table 2.1. Theoretical Perspectives on Economic and Institutional Change

Perspective	Source of Failure	Motivation	Process
Social Welfare	Markets	Achieve efficiency	Rational: Neutral social planner enforces efficient allocation of economic surplus
Distributional	Government	Obtain economic rents and votes	Rational: Legislative change in public sector in response to interest group pressure
Institutional	Institutions	Minimize transaction costs	Boundedly Rational: change rules of the game in relevant governing sector

In the post W.W. II period until the early 1970's, there was little effort to explain regulation or regulatory change in the U.S. political economy. Prevailing theories harked back to Adam Smith and were based on social welfare analyses. It was assumed that certain natural monopolies and externalities existed and that government regulation was a necessary fact of economic life. Producers were expected to resist regulation but analysts assumed that in a democratic society, consumers, assisted by government representatives, would operate as a counter-balance and an efficient equilibrium would be achieved. However, in the 1970's, investigations of economic problems in regulated industries indicated that rather than correcting market failure, regulation often contributed to it by creating or solidifying monopoly power. The evidence suggested that in many cases producers actively supported regulation. And rather than acting as neutral social planners who consistently achieve efficient economic outcomes, regulators and those who appointed them were often ineffective in protecting consumer interests. Economists argued that the source of the problem was too much regulatory intervention in private economic activities and that governments should rely on markets rather than administrative oversight to achieve economic goals.

While social welfare approaches helped economists explain the inefficiency they observed, they could not explain the process by which it came about. The political maneuvering that emerged in response to deregulation and economic restructuring also posed interesting theoretical challenges for political scientists. Turning to work on collective choice and collective action such as that of Arrow (1951), Black (1958), Buchanan and Tullock (1962), Downs (1957), Niskanen (1971), and Olson (1965), economists and political scientists sought new approaches to explaining political and economic outcomes. Two approaches developed: the distributional political economy approach with twin developments in economics and political science, and the institutional political economy approach, which straddles and in many ways seeks to reconcile the two disciplines.

1.1. *Distributional Political Economy*

1.1.1. *Economic Theories*

Stigler (1971) was one of the first economists in the late 20th century to attempt to explain why regulation might be expected to encourage monopoly. He argued that rather than avoid regulation, industry actively seeks regulation that is "designed and operated primarily for its benefit." Stigler builds on "capture" theories of regulation, Downs' (1957) notion of rationally ignorant voters, and Olson's (1965) theory of collective action, and applies standard economic concepts.[5] He conceptualizes a market for regulation with a demand side given by the interest of an industry to maximize profits by controlling entry, and a supply side given by the interest of political parties to maximize reelection of incumbent members by monopolizing political control. That is, self-interested political parties produce and sell regulation to equally self-interested regulation consumers (firms), in exchange for votes and other resources that advance party ambition. Both organization and information costs are important aspects of Stigler's analysis.

Stigler's main conclusion with respect to regulatory change was that in a given political contest between groups of disparate size, a relatively small, concentrated producer interest group is likely to achieve monopoly-enhancing regulation at the expense of a large, diffuse taxpayer group. The motivation for producers to seek change is to obtain excess economic profits. The process involves elected representatives and their parties finding a coalition of voter interest that is more durable than the anti-industry side of every industry proposal.

Stigler's work has been critiqued and extended by Posner (1971, 1974), who emphasizes the ability of consumer groups to achieve "internal subsidization," low or below-cost subsidies from excess profits generated elsewhere in the regulated industry. Peltzman (1976) demonstrates theoretically that as long as some consumers can offer some votes or resources for a small departure from the cartel equilibrium, pure producer protection will not generally be the dominant political strategy. Becker (1983) argues that represented groups should favor policy that maximizes economic surplus available for distribution among them. If all interests affected by a regulatory decision are represented with approximately equal effectiveness, the resulting policy is likely to be socially efficient. Posner (1971) argues that if all interests are not effectively represented, the policy is likely to create monopoly or oligopoly rents that are dissipated among the coalition members. In a critique of Peltzman's model, Weingast (1981) argues that the theoretical foundations for regulation, deregulation, and re-regulation are the same: special interest groups that exploit a fragmented policymaking system in order to maximize in-group benefits.

With respect to the process of change, economic theories of distributional political economy imply, but do not fully develop, a role for political entrepreneurs, political parties, and regulatory agencies. Theorists assume that elected officials

---

[5] The earliest articulation of capture theory of economic regulation is generally attributed to Bernstein (1955).

ultimately control regulatory decisions and that they seek to produce policy that satisfies the interests of groups in the private sector, which will provide critical resources for re-election in exchange for favorable policy decisions. Change may or may not be more efficient than the status quo, depending upon the distribution of preferences among politically important interest groups.[6]

A number of banking and finance economists have applied distributional political economy concepts to explain regulatory change in the banking industry. Havrilesky (1989) develops a model of banking regulation consistent with the Stigler-Peltzman approach in which exogenous change, such as a distributional or technological shock, results in shifts in political support and adjustments in the equilibrium level of regulatory barriers to entry and exit. The basic idea is that exogenous change reduces the benefits associated with a specific set of regulations. This reduction causes erosion in the political support participants give politicians. As a consequence, legislatures devise a new set of politically optimal regulatory arrangements.

Kane (1996) argues that recent changes in interstate banking regulation were driven by an irreconcilable struggle between regulators and banks. Political forces led regulators to impose and enforce rules that in some ways threatened to reduce the profits of banks. Banks struggled both politically and economically to make regulation less burdensome. Kane relies on a conflict model to explain the change process.[7] He then develops a formal rent-seeking model to explain the enactment of interstate banking regulation, arguing that geographic restrictions were not liberalized until technology and competitive regulatory enforcement created loopholes. In his view, these loopholes made it possible for banks to circumvent enough of the intended regulatory effects to reverse the pre-existing balance of lobbying pressure. Kane concludes that statutory change occurs when one or both of two things happen: (1) the customer-electorate has begun to lose faith in the social purpose of the statutes, or (2) activity to circumvent the rules has driven the protective value of existing rules to their proponents below the amount opponents are willing to pay for their removal.

There are also a number of empirical analyses of banking regulation that rely on distributional political economy approaches. Abrams and Settle (1993) apply a model of pressure group and rent seeking behavior to investigate the relaxation of twenty-two intrastate branching laws between 1931 and 1935. They argue that while high bank failure rates tipped the political balance toward pro-branching forces in many states, in a number of other states the growth of the influence of branch and group bankers and increases in urbanization were largely responsible for relax-

---

[6] For example, Joskow and Rose (1989) identify four types of regulatory redistributions: transfers to owners of regulated firms, transfers to factors of production, transfers among consumer groups, and transfers among producers.

[7] The "Regulatory Dialectic" model is fashioned after the Hegelian model of change (Kane 1981 and 1984). The net burden of exclusionary regulation corresponds to a Hegelian thesis and the regulatory avoidance it provokes is interpreted as a Hegelian antithesis. After a lag, the conflict leads to a synthesis of adaptive re-regulation. Each adapted re-regulation takes its turn as the thesis in a succeeding cycle of conflict and change.

ation of restrictions over branch banking. Calomiris and White (1994) see banking regulation as a function of bargaining within long-standing coalitions. In their study of the origins of federal deposit insurance, the authors focus on the structure of interest group demands and the political response to these demands.

Kroszner (1997) argues that the origins of intrastate and interstate banking regulation as well as the dual banking system itself are associated with demand for government finance. He attributes the demise of interstate banking regulation to a change in the interest-group equilibrium such that large banks (who generally favored regulatory change) were able to prevail against small banks (who generally resisted regulatory change). Krozsner and Strahan (1998) argue that intrastate and interstate barriers were removed more quickly in states in which large banks had more political strength than small banks. Integrating their evidence with Kane's (1996) argument that broad technological, legal, and financial innovations altered the costs and benefits of interstate banking regulation, they argue that the Stigler-Peltzman "private interest" theory of regulation explains interstate banking deregulation. Similarly, Calomiris (1993), Krozsner (1998), White (1986), and Benston (1983, 1986) have used distributional political economy concepts in their historical explanations of regulatory change in the financial services industry.

1.1.2. *Political Theories*

Like economic theories of distributional political economy, political theories of economic and institutional change assume that regulatory change is a by-product of the interaction of coalitions of politicians and firms that seek to maximize self-interested gains. Whereas economic theories tend to focus on the motivation for reform, political theories focus more on explaining the structure of government and the process of reform. Dahl and Lindblom (1953) provide an early argument that special interests dominate diffuse interests in American politics. This logic, applied to understanding the politics of economic regulation, inspired the concept of "iron triangles" of regulators, regulated industries, and key members of Congress, which are impervious to external pressure from more diffuse public interests.

Fiorina's 1977 study of legislative decision-making is another classic foundation of the distributional political economy approach. Based on an empirical study of electoral behavior at the district level, he argues that Congress creates, sustains and expands a network of bureaucrats, citizen organizations, and Congressional representatives that weakens party power, changes electoral behavior, and leads to uncoordinated political operations. The system works thus: Congress creates federal programs that produce "election credits." These credits deliver incumbency advantage because "bureaucrats" and "regulation" absorb voter anger about ineffective government, while Congress provides ameliorative constituent service. Federal bureaucracy provides cover for Congress by obfuscating accountability for policy effects. This results in particularistic, disorganized national policymaking that cannot be changed because Congress has no incentive to change it.

Consistent with this perspective but in work that takes into account a decade of regulatory change that conferred diffuse benefits at the expense of special interests, Wilson (1980) argues that regulation can be explained as a function of the distribution of costs and benefits of a policy issue, the behavior of those who control regulatory agencies (who have distinct motivations), and environmental factors such as economics, technology, and ideas. He speculates that the distribution of costs and benefits of a particular policy issue shape incentives. These incentives generate particular patterns of coalitions and influence activity, which in turn, produce policy. He explains the process of regulatory change based on the rise of "entrepreneurial politics," a process in which someone who serves as a representative of individuals and groups who are not directly involved in the policymaking process, mobilizes public sentiment and connects reform to widely shared values. McCubbins, Noll and Weingast (1987) look at the use of administrative procedures as instruments of political control.

Hammond and Knott (1988) have applied a distributional political economy perspective to develop a set of hypotheses about the stability of regulation in the financial services industry. Conceptualizing regulatory regimes as a solution to a private cartel facing a prisoner's dilemma, they argue that these regimes are inherently unstable because of technological, economic and legal change, heterogeneity, "fungibility,"and "permeability." Regulatory reform works as follows: given economic, technical, or legal shocks that alter the status quo of those in an industry and creates competition from outside the industry, self-interested political pressure will be exerted for deregulation. This pressure will have a "snowball" effect leading to more and more deregulation.

1.2. *Institutional Political Economy*

The institutional political economy approach is in its infancy in comparison to the social welfare and distributional political economy approaches, and in many respects, it is a reaction against these approaches that seeks to more closely align theory with what can be observed empirically. While institutional theorists use a variety of methods from multiple disciplines, including historical, legal, economic, and political analyses, they are all concerned with the relationship between institutional arrangements or the "rules of the game," and political and economic behavior. Combining economic and contractarian approaches, Buchanan and Tullock (1962) provided an early argument for focusing on the relationship between constitutional arrangements and political and economic outcomes. Vincent Ostrom [1971 (1987)] analyzes how U.S. constitutional arrangements facilitate large scale, polycentric decision-making on an adaptive basis. Generalizing from industrial organization theory, Mancur Olson (1965) develops an analysis of collective action in a large, heterogenous political economy. A number of institutional theorists use historical analyses combined with quantitative or game-theoretic analyses to discover how economic conditions interact with institutional arrangements to create incentives for choice behavior in particular decision settings, e.g. Alston, Eggertsson, and North, ed. (1996) and Bates, Greif, Levi, Rosenthal, and Weingast (1998).

There is very little scholarship in institutional political economy that directly addresses regulatory change or U.S. banking regulation. General theories of economic and institutional change use concepts from contracting theory to incorporate the interactive effects of price and institutional variables to explain political-economic adjustment and change.[8] Regulation is conceptualized as an incomplete, relational contract among groups that includes procedures by which participants may adjust their relations in response to situational change. The regulatory problem is to design a governance structure that will minimize the cost of coordination for a given set of conditions, while still satisfying an objective function. Buchanan and Tullock's (1965) analysis of constitutional design is an early and influential example of this approach. Extending Coase's work (1937, 1960), Williamson (1985, 1996) conceptualizes economic organization as a nexus of contracts and analyzes incentives for economizing on the costs of transacting created by different contractual arrangements. Based on extensive work on economic and institutional change in western history, North (1993) develops a general theory of institutional and economic change that combines transaction costs and a Schumpeterian response to change in relative prices to explain the motivation for change. Dixit (1996) builds on Williamson's and North's work to develop a transaction cost framework for analyzing economic policymaking.

Empirical studies of regulatory change from the institutional political economy perspective include Hurst (1982), Rabin (1986), Golden and Libecap, eds. (1994), and Vietor (1994), who use historical and legal analyses to explain regulatory change over long periods of U.S. history. They attribute change to the interaction of a number of political and economic variables. Vietor's work is illustrative. Analyzing regulatory change over the period 1920–1980, he attributes regulatory reform to changing economic and political conditions, technological innovation, policy failure, new ideas, and political entrepreneurship. Gilligan, Marshall, and Weingast (1989), who analyze the decision making rules involved in passing the Interstate Commerce Act of 1887, argue that in order to understand regulatory outcomes, it is necessary to consider how existing economic conditions and the rules of the game influence the preferences and activities of interest groups and legislators.

Institutional political economy studies that specifically focus on U.S. banking are particularly sparse. Richter (1989, 1990) relies on contracting theories to develop a principal-agent model of banking regulation, however, given the polycentric structure of U.S. governance arrangements, this approach has limited relevance for explaining U.S. banking regulation. Vietor's (1994) study of regulatory change in the U.S. includes banking regulation as one case that supports his general explanation. Seeking an explanation for the structure of banking regulation in the U.S. in the 19th century, Wallis, Sylla, and Legler (1994) argue that the way states taxed banks had important implications for the way states regulated banks, and that the way states regulated banks affected they way they taxed banks.

---

[8] While contracting theory has been used by theorists working from social welfare economics, distributional political economy, and institutional political economy perspectives, work that uses contracting theory – particularly principal-agency concepts – is sometimes described in the literature as "new institutional economics". See for example Moe (1984) and Richter (1989/90). Eggertsson (1990) distinguishes between "neoinstitutional" theories that retain but modify standard neoclassical assumptions, and "new institutional theories" that reject strictly rational optimization in favor of boundedly rational decision-making processes.

2. Gaps and Opportunities

Despite considerable experience and research effort, there are significant gaps in our theoretical understanding of the causes and processes involved in economic and institutional change in the U.S. economy in general, and in commercial banking in particular. Social welfare provides an important perspective on economic regulation and, as a policy analysis tool, continues to be useful for providing reasoned input into social decision processes.[9] However, it is not a promising basis for formulating theories of economic and institutional change. First, as a theory to explain the motivation for change, it is empirically suspect. Tests in the post World War II period provide evidence of policy change efforts both in the presence of market failure and in the absence of market failure.[10] Second, operationalizing the concept for a specific range of economic activities can be quite troublesome. This is because defining and measuring market failure requires extensive time series data for all enterprises in a given industry under a broad set of economic conditions (in order to control for business cycle effects). And, since most industries consist of a large number of privately and publicly held enterprises of differing sizes and sophistication operating in a variety of environments, it difficult to collect accurate and comprehensive data. One must also find a means to control for myriad sources of variability in operating performance.

Nor does the social welfare perspective provide a sound basis for explaining the process of institutional change. The technocratic process of rationally solving a constrained optimization problem bears little resemblance to observable social processes. The concept of a monocentric "neutral social planner" who calculates and solves regulatory dilemmas is theoretically and empirically inconsistent with the structure of decision making in liberal democratic political orders.[11] This inconsistency immediately limits its usefulness in describing regulatory change in many contemporary political economies. Moreover, it appears to be beyond human capacity to perform effectively as a neutral social planner: social psychologists and experimental economists have accumulated substantial evidence that human perceptual and cognitive abilities are subject to countless sources of fundamental attribution error.[12]

Distributional political economy theories offer useful critiques of theories of regulation that are based upon a social welfare perspective. By emphasizing the role of political competition and the process of making regulatory policy, these

---

[9] For thoughtful descriptions of the uses and limitations of social welfare economics in policy analysis, see for example, Stokey and Zeckhauser (1978) and Weimer and Vining (1992). For a discussion about generalizing from neoclassical economics, see Eggertsson (1990).

[10] For summaries of the evidence, see Noll (1989a).

[11] Arrow's Impossibility Theorem is a particularly elegant statement of this problem.

[12] There are any number of excellent introductory texts to social psychology and experimental economics that provide detailed descriptions of evidence that demonstrate the tenuousness of human cognitive capacity for rational decision-making. For a recent review of the experimental economics literature, see Camerer (1998). For a discussion and critique of the neoliberal rationality assumption in economics and political economy, see Simon (1959, 1986) and E. Ostrom (1998), respectively.

theories provide the interesting result that rational pursuit of self-interest in a democratic, market-based political economy can result in an inefficient distribution of economic surplus. However, this perspective has not produced a completely satisfying theory of either the motivation for change or the process of producing change. If economic regulatory behavior is motivated by the self-interested pursuit of rents and votes and the standard condition of nonsatiety is imposed, we should then expect to observe relatively constant levels of regulatory activity.[13] Instead, regulatory activity in the U.S., including de novo regulation, deregulation, and re-regulation, occurs intermittently and with variable intensity. For example, the vast majority of banking regulation activity in the 20th century has occurred in two periods: 1927–1935 and 1970–1999.[14] If we are to accept the distributional political economy perspective, we must explain why we pursue more rents and votes at some times in history than at other times.

While all those who have analyzed recent changes in U.S. banking regulation appear to agree that political activity was stimulated by changes in incentives, there is less agreement about which incentives changed and what caused them to change. Linkages between macroeconomic change and microeconomic change are implied but are not precisely specified. Havrilesky (1989) and Krozsner and Strahan (1998) emphasize the impact of innovation and technological change on the incentives of banks to pursue legislation that would protect them from competition. Without dismissing the impact of innovation and technological change, Kane focuses on the incentives of banks to change in response to regulatory enforcement activities. Hammond and Knott (1988) tie the incentive to change to competitive pressure arising from technological, economic, and legal changes.

Moreover, the empirical evidence does not appear to confirm the basic assumption of distributional political economy theories that political participants are rent seeking. This assumption is challenged by pro-competitive deregulation in industries that appeared to have been permanently captured by interest groups. Wilson (1980) can find no distinctive pattern of political influence in his case studies of a variety of regulatory change in the late 20th century. Derthick and Quirk (1985) and Vietor (1994) find that industry representatives sometimes seek regulation that is consistent with diffuse interests and inconsistent with maximizing their particular interests.[15] Empirical studies of change in U.S. banking suggest equally plausible alternative motivations, including adjusting to economic and institutional innovations, structural change, and maintaining a healthy and stable financial system.

Finally, while distributional political economy theories are less institutionally

[13] Utility theory assumes that preferences exhibit nonsatiety. That is, given a choice, one will always prefer the option that provides more of something desirable than less of this same thing: more is always better. Because there is no highest utility level or bliss point, this assumption has the important property that it rules out circular indifference curves.

[14] For examples in other regulatory areas see Weiss and Klass (1981, 1986) and Vietor (1994).

[15] In a particularly germane example, Vietor (1994) finds that in the late 1970s, Bank of America (the largest bank in the U.S. at the time) actively sought regulatory change that was not only inconsistent with maximizing their economic rents, but had legislation been passed, it would have resulted in immediate and serious financial damage to the bank.

sparse than social welfare theories, they are, nevertheless, underdeveloped. The U.S. constitution permits a wide range of countervailing forces to operate in political and economic systems, yet distributional theories of economic and institutional change focus primarily on the activities of interest groups, regulators, and legislators. Studies of U.S. banking overlook the relationship between change activities in the private sector and those in the public sector. This oversight limits the explanatory power of the distributional theories.

Institutional theories of regulatory change address gaps in social welfare and distributional political economy theories by emphasizing the interactive effects of a self-interested search for economic surplus, institutional arrangements that permit or constrain this search, and exogenous shocks, such as price changes, innovation, and so on. Considering changes in both the political-economic context and institutional constraints imposed on adjustment to these changes shows promise for helping to account for the ambiguous relationship between special interest political activity and economic policy outcomes. However, institutional theories have not been applied to explain changes in U.S. commercial banking or to any other similarly constructed change processes. While Gilligan, et al. (1989) link microeconomic, market structure, and interest group variables with the federal legislative process in their institutional analysis of passage of the Interstate Commerce Act, they do not consider other centers of influence such as the executive or judicial branches, or other levels of government such as the states. Nor does this analysis consider a policymaking situation in which there is an established regulatory regime or the ability to take private action that does not require regulatory change. Like distributional theories, institutional or "positive" theories of legislative behavior fail to consider the role of alternative decision-making processes in political and economic change.[16]

Even more troublesome are those institutional political economy theories that use principal-agent models to explain regulatory behavior.[17] The difficulty of conceptualizing a principal or an agent that is analytically tractable is suggested in V. Ostrom's [1971 (1986)] analysis of constitutional design, and the historical accounts of regulatory activity investigated by Commons (1968), Hurst (1982), Rabin (1986), and Vietor (1994): in polycentric systems, institutional change emerges from the interaction of multiple, rival contestants, which may not have single dimension preferences, and a number of overlapping decision processes.

Nevertheless, scholarship from all three perspectives provides a sound foundation for further studies of economic and institutional change. The social welfare perspective provides a rigorous framework for conceptualizing decision-behavior. By emphasizing the role of political processes as well as economic processes, the distributional political economy perspective highlights the role of a broad range of actors and the ways in which economic variables such as technology shocks

---

[16] For a review of these theories, see Shepsle and Weingast (1989).

[17] For a discussion and analysis of the difficulties of applying principal-agent models to explain U.S. policymaking, see Moe (1989). For an interesting critique of the principal-agent approach in the context of U.S. corporate law, see Clark (1983).

structure political competition for rents. The institutional political economy perspective leads us to reflect upon the role of the "rules of the game" in structuring information and incentives for adaptive decision-behavior. And work from both the distributional and institutional perspectives points to ways in which standard economic assumptions and can be modified to improve both explanatory power and predictability, such as by relaxing strict rationality assumptions and recognizing the effects of path dependence.

The next chapter builds on this foundation by developing an analytic framework that makes it possible to analyze recent economic and institutional change in the U.S. commercial banking industry, compare alternative explanations, and develop more powerful theories.

CHAPTER THREE

A Theory of Change and a Framework for Analysis

The main point to be taken from the survey in Chapter Two is that we do not understand as much as we could about economic and institutional change in banking in the United States. The theoretical literature in economics and political science attributes reform to economic change that disrupts the political "equilibrium," which leads to interest group competition and legislative change. Case studies of regulatory change in a variety of industries including banking, attribute the stimulus for interest group competition and legislative reform to a variety of factors including changes in economic and political conditions, technological innovation, policy failure, new ideas, and political entrepreneurship. However, the precise connection between these factors and the motivation to pursue specific types of institutional change has not been fully developed either theoretically or empirically. While scholarship in institutional political economy emphasizes the role of transaction costs and a broader range of institutional change processes than interest group competition and legislative activity, these theories have not been applied to explain banking reform in the late 20th century in the United States. In short, the linkages between economic change and institutional change have not been fully specified and the role of other governance processes has not been considered.

The incompleteness of the existing literature leaves us with a number of fundamental questions about economic and institutional change in regulated industries in the United States.

1. What stimulates change in a regulated industry? When efforts to change the status quo emerge, are they in response to a failure or to an opportunity? What is the source of the opportunity or failure – markets, governments, institutions, or something else?
2. What is the process of change, e.g. what types of economic and institutional changes are occurring and how are they associated? What is the role of competition? Who is involved, what are their motivations for making change and which processes do they use?
3. Finally, given the complexity of change, how do we go about studying it in a particular industry?

In order to address these questions systematically, they must be linked to what we know about the sources of economic and institutional change. This chapter addresses this need and builds a framework for studying change in regulated industries. The first section analyzes economic change. The second section examines institutional change. The final section integrates the analyses in the first two sections to build a general theory of change and a framework for analyzing change in a particular setting. In subsequent chapters, the framework is applied to investigate change in the U.S. commercial banking industry over the period 1960–2000.

Economic Change

Standard theories conceptualize economic change as a function of the intensity of a set of productivity-enhancing inputs. In the classic approach, Solow (1956, 1957) models change as a function of capital and labor, which are organized, supplied, and directed in the private sector, and a residual factor. Labor productivity changes with capital intensity and any additional change in productivity is attributed to a "shift" or "residual" factor. Solow attributed changes in the residual factor to changes in technical progress, which is an unexplained, exogenous phenomenon. The basic Solow model is:

$$Y = F(A, K, L),$$

where (Y) is change in income, (A) is the residual, (K) is capital, and (L) is labor.

Solow's insight regarding the role of technical progress in economic change combined with the empirical observation that U.S. firms invest significant amounts of money in research and development activities has led economic theorists to formulate technical progress as an endogenous factor in economic change. Romer's (1994) growth theory is a good example. Romer hypothesizes that technical progress depends upon knowledge. He formulates knowledge as a factor that is embodied in proprietary product and process designs, which interacts with the stock of general knowledge through the application of human capital (H). Self-interested, profit seeking activity involves applying human capital to improve the productivity of commercially oriented research and development (R). Physical capital (K) is an additional input. Romer argues that the interaction among these factors creates knowledge spillovers that change the stocks of general and specific knowledge, resulting in economic change. Romer's model is:

$$Y = F(R, K, H)$$

Both Solow's and Romer's approach to change assume that economic behavior is rational and that it takes place in a competitive environment that permits investors to realize a return on their investment that reflects risk and opportunity costs. While Romer's model may do a better job of explaining what we observe empirically in the United States than Solow's, both approaches leave a great deal unexplained. The empirical evidence suggests that economic change emerges from the interaction of a number of factors including physical resources, capital, research, technical progress, human capital, prior growth experience, market conditions, entrepreneurship, leadership, knowledge spillovers from geographic proximity among complementary activities, and organizations and public policies that create incentives to innovate.[1] Based on long-experience with economic change in developing countries, Kamarck (2001) argues that we do not yet understand the fundamental problems that must be solved in order to make and sustain economic change. In his view, we have not only failed to accurately account for the sources of growth, but the very assumptions upon which standard economic theories are based – self-interest, rationality, and equilibrium – are deeply flawed.[2] In other words, standard economic approaches are not able to fully explain the motivations and processes associated with change in real economic environments. If standard approaches do not fully explain economic change, what are some alternative approaches?

In the early decades of the twentieth century, economic scholars observed that large firms were increasingly important engines for change in market-based economies. However, from a theoretical perspective, it was not clear why firms existed at all let alone took different forms and sizes. In other words, why do some transactions occur at some times in markets and at other times within firms? And what accounts for changes in the governance structure and size of firms? Addressing himself to these questions, Coase (1937) argued that firms exist because, for a variety of reasons now typically associated with market failure, it is costly to transact in markets. Integrating transactions under managerial control (or spinning them back out into markets) is one way to change the governance structure of transacting and thereby reduce transaction costs.[3]

It logically follows from Coase's argument that any change that alters the direction of transaction costs stimulates firms to change the way that transactions are governed, which has a broader economic impact. As firms reorganize arrangements that govern transacting, economic structure changes and outcomes change. However, individuals establish rules and organize and manage the activities of firms, not economic optimization machines. So we need to look beyond the firm to understand why changes in transaction costs might motivate the individuals who manage firms to reorganize the way that economic activities are governed.

Focusing on the individual entrepreneur rather than the firm *per se*, Schumpeter [1947] (1976) developed an alternative but complementary theory of how economic change occurs in a market-based system. He attributes change to an evolutionary process, "creative destruction," in which a particular economic path is restructured as a function of how entrepreneurs respond to opportunities and threats that are likely to have a significant impact on the firm's competitive position. The driving force for change is real or perceived;

---

[1] For a concise overview of economic thought on growth and innovation, see F.M. Scherer (1999). For a review of the evidence on sources of growth, see Abramovitz (1993).

[2] For additional arguments and evidence related to developing countries, see World Bank Annual Reports (1997, 2000/2001, 2002) and Sen (2001).

[3] Note that in later work, Coase (1960) applies the concept of transaction costs to address governance problems associated with the provision and production of quasi-public goods and services.

"... competition which commands a decisive cost or quality advantage and which strikes not at the margins of profits and the outputs of existing firms *but at their foundations and their very lives* ..." (emphasis added).

In Schumpeter's analysis, individuals seek to protect a way of life as much as they do an economic return. Any change in competition that they believe provides an economic advantage or threatens the status quo – presumably this would include changes in the costs of transacting as well as production and distribution – stimulates them to make changes in the way that they do business. The primary means of responding to competitive challenges is organizational change, e.g. reorganizing procurement, production, distribution, sales and marketing, and so on.[4]

Building on Coase's work, Williamson (1985, 1996) develops a theory of economic performance based on transaction costs and institutions. He conceptualizes an economy as a nexus of contracts that are designed, negotiated, and enforced to mitigate contracting hazards. Williamson argues that economic performance can be explained by the extent to which the "mechanisms" employed to govern contract relations minimize transaction costs. Mechanisms that govern contracting relations are agreements and procedures that specify the persons who may participate in economic activity, the types of interaction they may engage in, and enforcement processes and penalties. These mechanisms are embedded in an "institutional environment," which includes higher level rules that specify and govern property rights and return on investment, the nature of economic relations, access, and participation, knowledge production, and collective action.

Extending Williamson's argument to explain economic change, one would expect to find an interaction between economic change and institutional change. Anything that changes transaction costs stimulates economic and institutional change. The source of this shock could arise in the economic environment or the institutional environment. Individuals and firms adjust by changing the mechanisms that govern contracting relations or the higher level rules in the institutional environment, such as regulation. Changes in contract governance or higher-level rules determine economic performance. The motivation for making change is to minimize transaction costs.

Similarly, North (1993, 1981) argues that there is a necessary interaction between economic and institutional change. Studying economic change in the western economies over very long time periods, North observes that economic change is

---

[4] In later work, Schumpeter argued that successful entrepreneurial firms would evolve into large, bureaucratic firms that would dominate and destroy entrepreneurial culture. While the growth in large firms in the U.S. in the post W.W.II period appeared to support Schumpeter's thesis, the explosive growth of small firms in the 1980s did not. In the late 20th century, scholars have questioned the extent to which managers are motivated to engage in economically rational behavior. The extensive work of Michael Jensen is illustrative. As a general rule, contemporary scholarship in managerial economics, which focuses on how firm governance and public policies create positive or perverse incentives for managerial behavior, takes an institutional perspective on economic and institutional change but at a micro level.

consistently associated with changes in technology and institutions, or "the rules of the game." North argues that prices are determined by transaction and production transformation costs, which are determined by technology and institutions. His idea is that economic activity generates costly coordination problems. Applying technology and changing the rules that govern coordination solves these problems. How these coordination problems are solved determines the degree of market uncertainty and the stability of economic activity. If cost minimizing solutions are implemented, economic performance improves. But in North's view, we cannot assume that self-interest automatically leads to economically optimal solutions. Economic activities are embedded in a larger institutional framework that enables and constrains adaptive change. While other theorists assume that the institutional environment for a given set of economic activities creates incentives to economize, North and Williamson draw our attention to the possibility that it may not or may do so imperfectly.

In summary, neoclassical theories assume that changes in factor prices are the primary incentive for economic change; however, these theories do not explain why or how factor prices change. New growth theories focus on advances in knowledge and innovation, which are thought to be self-generating: as the stock of knowledge changes, innovation changes, and economic change occurs. These theories do not explain why or how stocks of knowledge or innovation change. While recognizing the importance of the factor prices, knowledge, and innovation, theories in institutional economics focus on the beliefs of individuals, competitive conditions, transactions costs, and governance. Factor prices, knowledge, and innovation emerge from activities that are shaped by beliefs about the impact of external events and by incentives and constraints imposed by institutional arrangements.

The institutional explanation for economic change appears to conform to the empirical evidence a bit better than either the neoclassical or the endogenous growth explanation. Holding physical resources, stocks, flows, and prior economic experience constant, the evidence on sources of economic growth suggests that change depends upon changes in market conditions, changes in leadership and entrepreneurship, and changes in the way that individuals and firms organize economic activity in response to changes in market conditions. Institutions affect each of these variables by enabling, constraining, and creating incentives for action. Empirical studies of the price mechanism in U.S. manufacturing, which test neoclassical theories of price behavior, also support the institutional view of change. These studies find a strong role for both menu prices and administered prices.[5] Yet menu prices emerge from competitive market activity, which is governed by higher-level competition rules. Administered prices emerge from bi-lateral contracting activity, which is governed by contracts and other organizational arrangements. Contracting activity is governed by higher level commercial and property rights rules. Hence price change evidence implies that institutions that govern contracting activity and competition play key roles in price flexibility, which, in turn, is a necessary condition for

[5] For a summary of price studies, see Carlton (1989).

economic change. So in order to understand economic change, we need to understand institutional change, which is something that standard theories of economic change do not address.

Institutional Change

Theories and evidence on economic change suggest that economic performance depends upon institutional flexibility in as many as four different areas of activity in the private and public sectors: individual, firm, industry, and government. This implies that in order to understand the capacity for institutional change in a given setting, we need to understand how much latitude individuals, firms, industries, and governments have to alter institutions in a particular economic environment. In the United States, institutional change is subject to a written Constitution, which controls how occupants and territories are governed, and how individuals, firms, industries, and government may interact to change rules or adopt new routines.

Functionally, the U.S. Constitution is an agreement among otherwise sovereign states, ratified by the people of those states to form a union for the purpose of implementing the Declaration of Independence, which asserts the right of individuals to govern themselves in pursuit of their self-interest. The agreement, which consists of the Articles of Confederation and the Amendments, creates a federation of states, of which there are fifty, and guarantees the people of each of these states a republican form of government, protection against invasion, security of their liberties and properties, and their mutual and general welfare. Three co-equal branches govern the federal republic: the Executive branch, the Legislative branch (the U.S. Congress), and the Supreme Court. Federal powers include the authority to regulate taxation, money and standards of weights and measures, interstate commerce, immigration and naturalization, bankruptcy, post offices and roads, science, inventions, and intellectual property, constitute tribunals inferior to the Supreme Court, international relations, the union and sovereignty of the United States, and military affairs. Powers to act that are not delegated to the federal government by the Constitution are reserved for the states or the people. State constitutions, which follow the federal form of government by creating three co-equal branches of government and delegating powers to regional and local governing bodies, specify the institutional environment at the local level.

Key features of the U.S. institutional environment include:

- All citizens are free to act independently in pursuit of their self-interest and to associate with others and engage in collective action. However, all are equally subject to the rule of law, which limits the discretion of private and public authority.
- The legislative, executive and judicial branches of government are separate and equal, however, each branch can exercise veto power over the other, hence they are strategically interdependent.
- Legislation, which is made in many centers of government, is the product of

bargains that are struck by policy-makers who represent local, state and national interests: it can be challenged by those who are affected by it and interpreted by administrative and judicial rulings.
- Unless otherwise specified by the Constitution, policy on the same subject matter can differ between levels of government and across governments.
- The limited nature of the U.S. Constitution permits citizens to make alternative institutional choices, including changing the Constitution itself.

While the principle of decentralization of authority is a widely understood aspect of the U.S. institutional environment, the principle of polycentric authority is less understood but equally important. The Founders of the Republic were as concerned about the tyranny of democratically constituted majorities as they were of monarchies that ruled by divine right. To cope with this problem they constructed a system of checks and balances on the relative influence of individuals and groups that was intended to encourage the co-existence of many centers of private and public activity. The U.S. model of polycentric governance involves voluntary coordination among disparate centers of control based upon common interests and militates against the formation of large, centralized bureaucracies that exercise monopoly control.[6]

A polycentric system of governance allows participants to organize many different allocation mechanisms at different levels of authority and at different scales of activity. In a hierarchical system there is a single, final source of authority. By contrast, in a polycentric system, there are many sources of authority, which may compete or cooperate with respect to systemic issues depending upon the rules of the particular system, and no final source of authority. Banking oversight is a good example of polycentric governance: it involves ten federal agencies and fifty state agencies that regulate ten different types of financial service enterprises operating in twenty regulation-defined markets related to borrowing, transaction management, and savings.[7] In addition, while bank regulators have the authority to regulate bank structure, balance sheet composition, business activities, and pricing in their jurisdictions, their activities are subject to review by executive, legislative, and judicial branches of government as well as civil society.

An important implication of polycentric systems is that while collective action on a large-scale is possible, it is, by design, difficult to achieve. Madison 51 describes the framers' logic in fragmenting governing authority:[8]

---

[6] The concept of a polycentric political economy is described in Ostrom, Tiebout, and Warren (1961). Ostrom (1972) elaborates on the concept.

[7] For an overview of regulation-defined financial service markets that is relevant to the period of time covered by this study, see Vietor (1994).

[8] Following the Constitutional Convention, Alexander Hamilton, James Madison, and John Jay published a series of essays that have come to be called *The Federalist Papers*, in which they explained the logic of the Constitution and sought to build support for ratification. For a summary and analysis of debate about the framers' intent regarding the design of the republic and Madison 51 in particular, see Banning (1995).

"But the great security against a gradual concentration of the several powers in the same department, consists in giving to those who administer each department, the necessary constitutional means, and personal motives, to resist encroachments of the others . . . Ambition must be made to counteract ambition. The interest of the man must be connected with the constitutional rights of the place. It may be a reflection on human nature, that such devices should be necessary to controul the abuses of government. But what is government itself but the greatest of all reflections on human nature? If men were angels, no government would be necessary. If angels were to govern men, neither external nor internal controuls on government would be necessary. In framing a government which is to be administered by men over men, the great difficulty lies in this: You must first enable the government to controul the governed; and in the next place, oblige it to controul itself. A dependence on the people is no doubt the primary controul on the government; but experience has taught mankind the necessity of auxiliary precautions. This policy of supplying by opposite and rival interests, the defect of better motives, might be traced through the whole system of human affairs, private as well as public."[9]

The success of the Federalists in designing a stable government in which authority is both decentralized and fragmented has produced a vexing puzzle for those who analyze institutional change in the United States. Observing the difficulty of achieving large-scale collective action, Mancur Olson (1965) developed a theory that has influenced scholarship in both distributional and institutional political economy. He argued that small groups can easily coordinate and use the mechanisms of government to satisfy common interests but large groups will not be able to do so without "special institutions." Conceptualizing political influence as a market for a public good, Olson argued that as the size of a group increases, the rate of change of the cost of influence exceeds the rate of change of the benefit of influence such that it is not rational to act to change institutional arrangements. Instead, it is rational to refrain from action and "free-ride" on the effort of others. When the benefits of free riding exceed the costs, there is no incentive to pursue change and the status quo will prevail.

Vincent Ostrom has a different perspective on collective action in the United States than Olson. Analyzing the theoretical principles upon which the U.S. Constitution is based ([1971], 1987; 1994), he argues that the real centers of influence and control in the U.S. political economy are located outside of formal government. Moreover, many of those who founded the republic did not believe that large-scale collective appeals to government to solve coordination problems were either desirable or necessary.[10] Reflecting upon the Federalists' notion of a "compound republic," Ostrom characterizes the United States as a polycentric, rule-ordered configuration of "shared communities of understanding." These com-

---

[9] From Cooke, Ed., 1961.

[10] Thomas Jefferson is perhaps the best known and most widely cited of this group.

munities, which can be business or civic enterprises, are voluntary, self-governed associations based upon common interests and compatible norms. In his view, institutional change that originates in these communities is more likely to effectively solve coordination problems than change that originates in legislatures or other governmental bodies, which have less knowledge of local circumstances.[11]

While Olson and Ostrom use different methods and arrive at different perspectives on institutional change in the United States, the practical implication of their analyses is quite similar: institutional change arises from common interests and is as likely to be found in relatively small, locally concentrated associations as in legislatures, regulatory agencies, executive offices, or courts. Hence, if we wish to understand institutional change in the U.S., we must first investigate how economic and institutional events affect the interests of individuals; second, how the institutional environment affects the incentives of these individuals to satisfy their interests; and third how the institutional environment enables or constrains them in associating with others to satisfy common interests. More generally, we must understand collective action problems and the rules that pertain to solving these problems in the private and public sectors.

Integrating Economic and Institutional Change

Table 3.1 summarizes theories and evidence on economic and institutional change. The empirical evidence suggests that any number of factors may stimulate change and that the process of change has something to do with how these factors interact. Standard economic theories, including neoclassical and new growth theories, focus on changes in factor prices, technical progress, knowledge, innovation, and productivity. Coase and Williamson approach change through the lens of the economics and organization of transacting. Schumpeter emphasizes changes in individual beliefs about the impact of competition and organizational change. Those who focus on the process of institutional change, such as Olson and Ostrom, emphasize changes in self-interest and collective action. North (1993) integrates ideas from standard economics and institutional economics, arguing that economic and institutional change arises from changes in relative prices that alter the bargaining strength of rivals and creates an incentive for entrepreneurial individuals to bear the costs of making institutional change. Price changes must be of sufficient magnitude that the expected benefits of institutional change are greater than the cost of pursuing change. Intermediary organizations may also participate in the process.[12]

---

[11] Ostrom's analysis does not preclude institutional change that either usurps the prerogatives of voluntary associations or creates disincentives for self-governed activity. In later work (Ostrom, 1997) he analyzes the erosion of these principles in American political and economic life.

[12] In the context of Olson's argument, North's "intermediary organizations" can be construed as "special institutions," which help relatively large groups overcome collective action problems.

Table 3.1. Theories and Evidence on Economic and Institutional Change

Source	Stimulus	Process Focus
Solow	• Change in price of factor inputs • Technical progress	Productivity
Romer	Change in stocks of knowledge	Innovation
Coase	Change in transaction costs	Organization
Schumpeter	Change in beliefs about the impact of competition	Creative destruction/Organization
Olson	Change in interests	Collective action
Ostrom	Change in interests	Self-governed action
Williamson	Change in transaction costs	Minimize transaction costs by changing: • Contracting mechanisms • Institutions
North	Change in relative prices	Institutions
Empirical evidence (Abramovitz, Carlton, Scherer)	Change in: • Prices • Factor inputs, including human capital and stocks of knowledge • Physical resources • Prior economic experience • Market conditions • Entrepreneurship • Leadership • Organization • Institutions	Interaction of factors

Combining the foregoing theoretical and empirical insights gives us a general theory of change. Holding constant many of the situational factors the empirical literature identifies, e.g. physical resources, prior economic experience, entrepreneurship, leadership, etc., and given an economic or institutional shock such as technological change, a change in demand, or a change in the rules of the game, economic and institutional change is a dynamic, adaptive response (Δ), which is a function of beliefs (B) about competitiveness; governance (G), which interacts with the institutional environment by creating incentives for individual and collective action by way of rules pertaining to participation, access, authority, decision making, scope, information, payoffs or consequences, and enforcement; and economizing (E), which interacts with the economic environment and represents a particular configuration of economic factors and production processes:

$$\Delta = F(B, G, E)$$

This model incorporates change in four areas: changes in beliefs begin with individuals who may exert influence in other sectors, changes in governance and economizing are located in the enterprise, changes in the economic environment occur in the industry, and changes in the institutional environment occur in government.

Stylized, change works something like this. Given a development in either the economic or institutional environment that challenges the beliefs of individuals about opportunities and threats, depending upon the types of individuals in the situation, e.g. their personality structures and norms, they will either change their beliefs or not. If they change their beliefs, they may then revise the contracting mechanisms they use to govern their transactions and the configuration of economic transformation activities. The changes they implement will be circumscribed by 1) their individual abilities to generate and select from an array of alternatives that are adaptive and then effectively implement these changes, 2) regulation and other pertinent rules of the game, and 3) economic resources.

If individuals lack the ability to implement change and fail to solve the collective action problems related to associating with others who have complementary abilities, their enterprises will fail to adapt. At the same time, if otherwise capable individuals are either prohibited from making change or the likely consequence or return on investment is insufficient to provide an incentive to change, their enterprises will fail to adapt unless they solve the collective action problems related to changing the rules of the game. Finally, even if individuals are capable, the rules permit change, and their incentives are aligned, if they do not have access to the resources required to implement change, their enterprises will fail to adapt. Figure 3.1 illustrates this idea.

The concept of transaction costs allows us to integrate these ideas about economic and institutional change into standard models of change. Just as factor prices are a means to measure the cost of alternative configurations of transformation activities and alternative economic environments, transaction costs are a means to measure the cost of alternative governance mechanisms, which in turn, reflect the cost of alternative institutional environments and the beliefs of participants about compe-

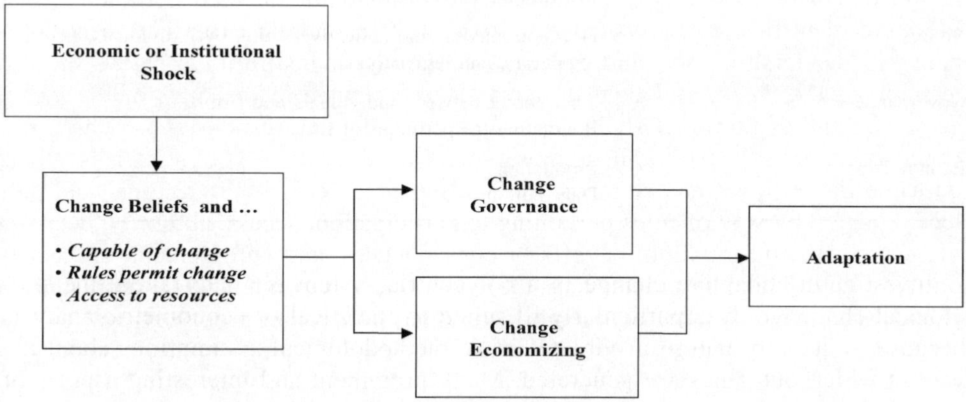

Figure 3.1. Economic and Institutional Change.

tition and the need for change. Incentives to minimize transaction costs are embodied in the mechanisms that govern managerial activities. These incentives are determined by owners of firms and regulators, as well as in the rules of the game that govern competition, commercial, and property rights rules, which are determined outside specific firms and industries by legislative, executive, and judicial authority. We can incorporate this idea in standard models of change by adding an additional term to represent transaction costs (T), which yields:

$$\Delta = F(B, G, E) \rightarrow Y = F(A, K, L, T) \text{ or } Y = F(R, K, H, T)$$

We now have a theory that provides a framework for systematically analyzing change in a regulated industry in the U.S., such as banking. Economic and institutional change is an adaptive process that involves four types of simultaneous change, which are located in multiple areas of activity. Empirical investigation must address the following questions:

1. Is there change in the economic or institutional environment that creates new opportunities or threatens the status quo in the industry?
2. How do changes in the economic or institutional environment affect beliefs about the competitive situation?
3. In responding to change, what are the collective action problems and in which sector(s) do they reside?
4. What changes in economizing are observable?
5. What institutional changes are observable and in which sectors do they occur? What happens to transaction costs?

Table 3.2. Investigating Change

Type of Change	Location of Activity
Competitive Shock	• Economic Environment • Institutional Environment
Beliefs	• Decision making and collective action by individuals, firms, regulators, and legislators
Governance	• Transacting between individuals and firms • Regulating the activities of firms
Economizing	• Production • Distribution

Investigating adaptive change in a polycentric system is a substantial methodological challenge. It is particularly ill suited to statistical or econometric analysis because by its very nature, it violates basic methodological assumptions about the way in which outcomes are generated. Many prominent and interesting aspects of the relationships in these systems are potential sources of endogeneity in a statistical model. At times policy makers are independent and at other times they are interdependent. There is more than one policy maker in a polycentric system and in some circumstances (but not all) the actions of one policy maker can affect the actions of other policy makers. Policy outcomes for a particular member in the system depend upon not only the strategies chosen to implement individual preferences, but also on the strategies chosen by other members of the system to implement their preferences. Moreover, interaction between individuals in the system holds evolutionary potential. As policy makers interact, they have the opportunity to learn from each other's experience as well as their own. In addition to fostering replication, this interaction provides the opportunity to discover entirely new solutions to policy problems.

To further complicate the analysis, the theory of change investigated in this study suggests that change is a path-dependent, dynamic choice made by individuals who are boundedly rational.[13] Policy makers take an action at time t, influenced by actions that took place at time $t - 1$, knowing that subsequent actions must be taken at time $t + 1$, $t + 2$, $t + 3$, and so on. Actions taken at time t have an impact on either how the policy maker views later choices or what choices will be available in the future or both. This would be a relatively straightforward dynamic programming problem if policy makers had stable preferences consistent with a von Neumann-Morgenstern expected utility function and could rely upon a fully informed neutral social planner with perfect optimizing capabilities to coordinate among participants over policy outcomes. However, a polycentric system has no central planner. Policy choices are potentially subject to veto by other policy makers. Real policy choices are often difficult to measure and compare. Moreover, policy making is only part of the solution – the other part is implementation, which requires an entirely different set of social and technological capabilities. And as if these complications were not enough to confound systematic analysis, policy makers are linked to polities, which influence their choices in nontrivial ways.

The best methodological guidance for studying economic and institutional change comes from studies in contemporary institutional political economy where scholars are developing theories that take into account the fact that despite the foregoing complications, humans have demonstrated the ability to successfully adapt over time. These scholars typically employ a detailed analysis of events and outcomes in order address theoretical questions that are not easily handled by existing models.[14] A similar approach is taken in this study, which incorporates historical, qualitative, quantitative, and decision-theoretic analyses to address the theoretical questions

---

13 For a survey of what has been learned about rationality in individual decision-making, see Camerer (1998). For an early exposition on bounded rationality, see Simon (1959).

14 For example, in her long-term research program on the institutional structures of public economies and common pool resources, E. Ostrom has incorporated formal methods of analysis after inferring principles from extensive field research. Bates, Greif, Levi, Rosenthal, and Weingast (1998), who study a variety of problems in political economy, espouse a method of analysis that they call "analytical narratives," which integrates case studies with game-theoretic or rational choice reasoning. All of the essays in a volume on the political economy of institutional change edited by Alston, Eggertsson, and North (1996) rely on historical analyses to generate hypotheses. Most rely on case studies and descriptive statistical analyses to support their arguments.

in this chapter as they apply to economic and institutional change in the U.S. commercial banking industry in the late twentieth century. Chapter Four analyzes economic change in the industry and Chapter Five analyzes institutional change. These analyses provide an empirical basis for further speculation about the adaptive capacity of the U.S. banking system in Chapter Six.

CHAPTER FOUR

Economic Change 1960–2000

In this and the following chapter, the framework that is developed in Chapter Three is applied to analyze economic and institutional change in the U.S. commercial banking industry in the late 20th century. This chapter focuses on economic change. Section One, which provides background, describes the commercial banking business in the United States, including products, services, and markets. Section Two analyzes changes in the economic environment that affect beliefs about competitive opportunities and threats in the financial services industry. Section Three analyzes change in the commercial banking industry, which reflects changes in beliefs about competition that emerge as a consequence of change in the economic environment, and Section Four summarizes and concludes.

The U.S. Commercial Banking Business

Commercial banks are the largest class of banks in the U.S. financial services industry.[1] Along with other banks, they are exclusively empowered by either state or federal charter to take deposits and to originate loans: no other type of financial entity may function as both a depository and lending institutions. Banks' chief role in the U.S. financial system is credit allocation, which they have a duty to achieve through safe asset transformation. Collecting deposits from customers with a surplus of funds and making loans to customers with funds deficits, they transform short-term liquid liabilities into relatively long-term illiquid assets. Their ability to safely convert illiquid assets to money on demand a low cost on a very large scale has played a key role in facilitating consumption and capital investment in the U.S. economy.

A key implication of banks' authority to take deposits and make loans is their effect on the money supply. Employing a fractional reserve system, banks retain less than 100% of deposits in reserve, and hence they create money when they make a loan. To fulfill this function, commercial banks collect and process information and manage risk – credit risk, interest rate risk, and exchange rate risk. In short, they

[1] Other major classifications of banks include savings and loans (thrifts) and credit unions.

assume risk, pool risk, price risk, and trade risk. This means that banks must maintain adequate capital to cover their risks and monetary policymakers must be alert to the effects of interest rate adjustments on the incentives of bankers to exercise prudence in managing their funds. It also means that banking has a systemic character and therefore a quasi-public economic nature.

The quasi-public aspects of banking arise not only from the ability of banks to create money when they make loans, but also from the externalities involved in banking activities.[2] Banks that do not properly price their products and services or safely manage the risks associated with their activities run the risk of failing. The failure of one bank can touch-off a banking panic, which can lead to system-wide financial crisis and severe macroeconomic pressure.[3] In other words, the actions of any one bank are linked to the actions of other banks so that bank activities have externalities. Because banks might not take this externality into account in pricing risk and determining the amount of private capital to invest, the socially optimal capital ratio for an individual bank may be greater than the privately optimal ratio and some form of systemic coordination is required to protect macroeconomic stability.[4]

The public nature of the banking business has been widely recognized since its inception in the United States. The earliest American banks were chartered because they were considered as "some sort of public utility," or in the more mystical terminology of the 18th and 19th centuries, "public blessings."[5] And banks are still widely regarded to have unique functions that distinguish them from other financial services firms, and hence justify subsidies in the form of discounted borrowing, protections in the form of federally guaranteed deposit insurance, and extensive regulation of management decision-making and control.[6]

The profitability of a bank depends principally upon the interest spread between what it pays depositors and what it collects from borrowers, less the costs of doing business. At one time, commercial banks focused on loans to business. Other large loan concentrations include mortgage and consumer loans. Returns on securities, purchased as a means of earning interest on assets and diversifying portfolio risk, are another source of earnings. Fee-generating activities from asset management and

---

[2] Kindleberger [1978] (1996) makes a similar argument in analyzing the role of money and credit mechanisms in financial crises.

[3] For a complete analysis of the systemic risk of banking activities, see Diamond and Dybvig (1983).

[4] Since the benefits of system-wide stability accrue to all economic actors, not just to bank owners, it may not be socially or economically appropriate to have only bank owners bear the costs. This potential negative externality provides the justification for government intervention to provide a safety net (Kroszner, 1998).

[5] The most frequently cited public benefits of banking in early charters and related documents included the capacity to make loans to government, to create an additional medium of exchange, to aid in assuring a sound currency, and to support the expansion of commerce and trade (Redlich, 1968).

[6] Corigan (1982) identifies three special services: 1) banks offer transaction accounts; 2) banks are the backup source of liquidity for all other economic institutions; and 3) banks are the transmission belt of monetary policy. Modern banking texts enumerate similar characteristics. For a critical analysis of these suppositions, see Saunders (1988).

trade-related services such as currency exchange, interest rate swaps, transaction processing activities, and so on, are an increasingly important source of income.

The principal activities of commercial banks are to collect deposits, make loans, and to manage money. Deposits are recorded as liabilities on banks' balance sheets: loans and investments are recorded as assets. Deposits are the main source of banks' funds for lending. Lending and asset management are the main sources of banks' earnings. Banks' assets are derived from a variety of activities including commercial, consumer, and real estate lending, investment, and trading. Commercial and industrial loans (C&I) usually involve large dollar amounts. They can be made on a short, medium, or long term basis and they can be either secured or unsecured. Processing costs are relatively low for C&I loans. Pricing, including interest rates and fees, is flexible. The market for C&I loans and deposits is based on relationships that commercial bankers build with business owners, corporate Directors and Officers, and financial managers. Once a low-risk and profitable line of business, today competition for C&I loans is quite high and yields are often relatively low.

Consumer loans, including installment and credit card lending, are usually small-dollar volume loans that are medium-term in maturity with predictable principal and interest payments. Consumer loans may be secured by real property such as an auto loan, or unsecured, such as a credit card loan. Credit risk and processing costs are generally higher for consumer loans than for business loans and yields can be subject to usury ceilings in some states. While bankers still cultivate private banking relationships with customers with high net worth, the market for consumer loans and deposits is primarily based upon mass-marketing to a wide variety of credit-worthy customer groups. The consumer lending business is intensely competitive.

Commercial and residential real estate loans are large dollar-volume loans and they are generally structured as long-term installment mortgages secured by a borrower's property. Residential mortgages are relatively low-risk and generate a predictable cash flow. Commercial real estate loans and interim construction loans are medium-term loans that generate high yields and carry high risks. The market for commercial real estate loans is like the C&I market in that it is based upon relationships bankers build with business decision-makers who are involved in commercial real estate transactions, particularly real estate developers. Residential real estate loans are marketed like consumer loans. Commercial and real estate lending are highly competitive.

The other large class of assets that contribute to commercial banks' earnings is investment securities (taxable and tax-exempt bonds). Banks purchase securities as a means of earning interest on assets while maintaining liquidity to meet transaction demand. Investing in securities is also a means to diversify a bank's risk, improve the overall quality of its earning assets portfolio, and help manage interest rate risk. Securities are a particularly important source of earnings when lending is weak but ample funds for investing are available. The value of an investment security is typically based on the interest rate it receives. Hence, the values of investment securities fluctuate with the market level of interest rates. The maturities of these instruments vary. Municipal bonds usually have a longer term structure and are less liquid than U.S. government and Treasury bonds. However, earnings on municipals are tax-exempt, which makes them desirable for reducing taxable income and improving net earnings. Banks also hold trading account securities for realizing capital gains. These securities carry a higher risk so prudent management practice is to hold them in smaller quantities.

Finally, commercial banks derive earnings from non-interest income which includes service charges on deposit accounts and fees from other money management activities such as trust and custodial activities, mortgage banking, credit card lending, foreign currency transactions, check and securities processing, net gains and losses from trading activities, and so on. Historically, banks have derived a relatively small proportion of revenue from non-interest income. However, in recent years, this has become an attractive area for revenue growth because it is typically more stable than lending. Non-interest income sources do not follow loan growth cycles, hence they provide a revenue offset when loan activity slows. Moreover, fee-based revenues do not have the credit costs associated with lending activities.

Commercial banks' principal liabilities are demand and time deposits (consumer and business), foreign deposits and borrowings, negotiable certificates of deposit (CDs), federal funds, other short-term borrowings, long-term debt, and shareholders' equity. Demand and time deposits include checking accounts, regular savings accounts, money market and negotiable order of withdrawal (NOW) accounts, and six-month money market certificates. Interest rates paid on these accounts vary with money market interest rates. The rate that banks pay must be competitive in order to attract and retain depositors. Historically, these types of deposits have been stable and important sources of funds for banks and they are the least expensive way of funding loan growth. When deposit growth is slow, banks are forced to rely on more expensive funding sources such as borrowing funds at wholesale rates or liquidating investment securities portfolios.

Commercial banks serve many different markets and they have equally diverse sources of earnings. In general, there are two types of commercial banking in the U.S.: retail banking and wholesale banking. Traditionally, retail banking services include deposit accounts, nationwide checking, loan products, and credit cards. Retail banking is locally-oriented and must be tailored to suit the needs of household and local business consumers. On the retail side of commercial banking, a bank must be able to attract, retain, and process large volumes of small, relatively standard transactions. Wholesale banking is based upon business and government services and it is nationally and internationally oriented. Services include cash management, loan products, and alternative financial products. Wholesale banking requires the ability to attract, retain, and process relatively small volumes of large, complex transactions.

Most commercial banks engage in both retail and wholesale banking. This means that banks must develop effective strategies for marketing and pricing diverse products and services, optimizing diverse processing activities, and transacting in different geographic areas. There are four ways banks have organized to provide services: community banking; money center banking, regional banking; and banking through bank holding companies. Community banks typically have less than $500 million in assets and serve distinct communities or specialize in certain lines of business. Money center banks are very large and can serve a broader customer group than can smaller banks. Their size permits them to realize economies of scale in providing more complex financial services that require access to very sophisticated markets. A few of the largest money center banks concentrate almost entirely on wholesale banking, engaging in large trades and foreign exchange activities, a variety of risk management activities for corporate clients, and securities underwriting activity. Regional banking organizations operate like money center banks but focus on a regional service area. Bank holding companies own or have controlling interest in one or more banks.

In 1960 there were 13,126 commercial banks operating in the United States. Most commercial banking was conducted through community and money center banks rather than branch banks.[7] Despite the highly fragmented structure of U.S. banking, bankers enjoyed a quiet life. A thicket of regulation, which limited entry, geographic expansion, and product diversification, provided a considerable degree of protection and certainty. Throughout the 1950s, the commercial banking industry consistently returned 1% on total assets to shareholders who were either like-minded institutional investors or individuals with high net worth. And bankers could look forward to double-digit growth in earnings and income: in 1960, pre-tax net operating income increased 13% over the prior year and total income increased 11%.

However, by 2000, the economics of the commercial banking business had changed substantially. The majority of banks were still organized as community banks however the industry had consolidated to 8,315 commercial banks. Today, financial services holding companies and non-bank competitors dominate banking activities. The regulations that bankers faced in 1960 have been liberalized to permit them to branch across state lines and to offer a broader range of products and services. By 2000, most banks were branching rather than unit banks.[8] However, despite consolidation, banks face increasingly competitive markets dominated by larger and more diverse competitors. The balance of this chapter is devoted to examining changes in the economic environment and the impact of these changes on the industry.

Changes in the Economic Environment

In the late 1960's and early 1970's, a number of developments in the domestic and international environment affected the economics of banking in the U.S. economy, resulting in sharp changes in the relative prices of money and informa-

---

[7] Of the 13,126 banks operating in 1960, 10,740 were unit banks (operating only one office) and only 2,386 were branch banks (operating more than one office). Source: FDIC (2002).

[8] Of the 8,315 banks operating in 2000, 5,669 were branch banks and 2,646 were unit banks. Source: FDIC (2002).

tion processing, two key inputs in financial intermediation. The more prominent of these developments include high levels of government spending on the Vietnam War and the Great Society programs, which created large government debt and deficits and stimulated applied research in information and communication technologies; the formation of the Organization of the Petroleum Exporting Countries (OPEC), which created oil price shocks; the demise of the Bretton Woods exchange rate regime, which destabilized monetary policy; liberal international trade and anti-trust regimes, increased foreign investment by U.S. firms, and rapid growth in the European and East Asian economies, which changed the terms of trade for U.S. firms. The net effect of these developments was to create pro-competitive pressures in the U.S. political economy, which encouraged deregulation and the entry of foreign firms, monetary and fiscal policy experiments to control inflation and to ease structural adjustment, and rapid scientific discovery and technological innovation.

By the late 1970's the U.S. faced the unprecedented and theoretically unpredicted problem of "stagflation", the simultaneous existence of stagnating economic growth and inflation. Annual productivity growth slumped from 2.6% in the 1960–1968 cycle to zero in the 1973–1979 cycle, while the annual change in inflation ranged from 1.4% to 4.7% over the 1960–1968 cycle and from 8.7% to 13.3% over the 1973–1979 cycle.[9] Fiscal policy was quite liberal, the U.S. trade deficit increased and the economy began to restructure away from traditional sources of strength in agriculture, manufacturing, and industrial production toward service activities. As the level of debt and deficits rose, the U.S. became a debtor nation in the international financial system rather than a creditor nation. The value of the U.S. dollar fell against the currencies of nations with stronger economic fundamentals, such as Japan and Germany. Because of the importance of the U.S. economy in the world economy, there was increasing international pressure to improve U.S. economic fundamentals. Smarting at a perceived loss of competitiveness, domestic pressure for reform built as well.

In response to these developments the Board of Governors of the Federal Reserve instituted a tight monetary policy in the late 1970s that led to a sharp increase in the price of money. This policy produced a long period of volatility in the short-term interest rate, which is used in this analysis as a proxy for the price of money.[10] Over the period 1960–2000, the short-term interest rate varied from a low of 2.95% per annum in 1960 to a high of 14.07% in 1981, falling to 5.83% in 1987, and then increasing to 8.11% in 1988. It is particularly volatile over the period 1977–1987. After 1988, the rate fell, reaching a low of 3% in 1993. After 1993,

---

[9] The source for productivity data is The Economist (1992) and for inflation data, the U.S. Department of Labor, Bureau of Labor Statistics, CIP-U, 1913-Present, July 19, 2002.

[10] The short-term interest rate as measured by the 3-month Treasury bill rate, influences the cost of both debt and equity finance. It affects competition in financial services by increasing uncertainty about the cost of funds while simultaneously increasing pressure to manage return on investment. These dual pressures stimulate a search for financial substitutes with better price-performance trade-offs.

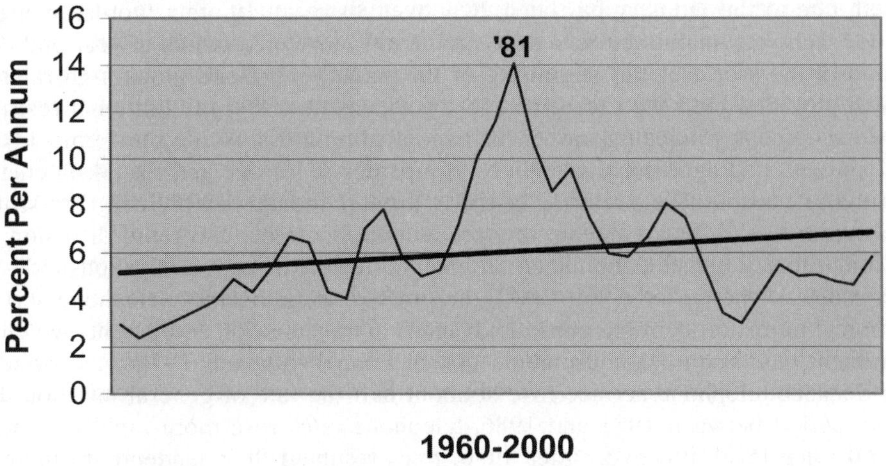

Figure 4.1. Short-Term Interest Rate.

Source: Author's estimate based on Federal Reserve statistics. Also see data appendix A1.

the rate is increasing, reaching 5.82% in 2000. Fitting a linear trend line to the data, over the period 1960–2000, the rate increases from approximately 5% to 7%.

Whereas the price of money was primarily affected by monetary and fiscal policy stances, the price of information processing, which can be approximated by observing changes in the cost of computing and the price of long-distance telephone service, was primarily affected by the competitive effects of technology shocks and liberal trade policies. As the terms of trade turned against the U.S. in industrial and manufacturing sectors and its international competitors gained domestic market share in industry stalwarts such as autos, electronics, and steel, the federal government stepped up funding for applied research in the emerging information and communications technology industries.[11]

The rapid growth in the computer hardware and software industries was driven in large part by technological progress in developing and manufacturing semiconductors, which made it possible to store and manipulate increasingly large volumes of data at increasingly rapid speeds. The magnitude of this progress is truly remarkable. In 1965, Gordon Moore, a founder of Intel Corporation, predicted that Intel would be able to double the number of transistors they could load on a single chip (and hence the processing power of microchips) every eighteen months for an indefinite period of time. Over the past thirty years, "Moore's Law" has fared quite well: the minimum feature size has been cut in half every six years, resulting in a 20-fold improvement in computing performance.[12] At the same time, the average price of a transistor has dropped almost six orders of magnitude while the annual

[11] For an analysis of the U.S. response to changes in competitive conditions in the late 20th century, see Board on Science, Technology, and Economic Policy and the National Research Council (1999).

[12] Moore (1997).

growth rate in the industry has been 20% over 30 years. In other words, over this period, each year manufacturers were producing more electronics at year end than existed in the world at the beginning of the same year. Continuous high rates of growth provided both the incentive and the means to invest in additional research and development, producing further technological progress. At the same time, liberal trade policies and aggressive growth by companies in Europe and East Asia created continuous competitive pressure in the computer industry, which further stimulated research and development, new product applications, and rapid diffusion.

Similar forces in the economic environment affected the communications industry. Over much of the period 1960–2000, the price of long-distance telephone service fell in real terms, reflecting technical advances in transmission equipment, switching equipment, and terminal equipment.[13] During the 1960s and 1970s, the price of long-distance telephone service rose at about half the rate of general inflation. For a brief period between 1981 and 1986, telephone rates rose more rapidly than the general price level, however, after 1986, rates resumed their tendency to increase much less rapidly than the general rate of inflation.[14] Thanks to interrelated advances in computing and telecommunications and a pro-competitive regulatory environment, the price of information processing fell in real terms. Changes in the relative prices of information processing combined with volatility in the price of money greatly altered the competitive playing field in the commercial banking industry.

Changes in Competition

Changes in competition in an industry are typically attributed to a number of interrelated factors including the number and diversity of competitors, factor prices, technological change, entry and exit barriers, expected growth rates, differentiation, and the magnitude of fixed costs, storage costs, and switching costs.[15] Over the period 1960–2000, changes in the relative prices of money and information processing reconfigured the number and diversity of competitors in the U.S. commercial banking industry, entry barriers, the price-performance tradeoff of substitute products and services, growth rates in key business segments, and the cost structure of back and front office activities.

---

[13] A host of inter-related technological innovations in the post-W.W.II period made these advances possible. Microwave technologies made it possible to transmit signals over the electromagnetic spectrum by microwave equipment and satellites. Advances in fiber optics technologies made it possible transmit signals through large coaxial cables, and advances in radio-based equipment have made it possible to construct complex cellular networks. Developments in electronics technologies revolutionalized telephone switching and terminal equipment while creating demand for new voice, data, and record services. Electronic photo-imaging technologies made it possible to create facsimile machines that allow documents to be transmitted over telephone lines. Modems and a variety of other equipment make it possible to transmit data over telephone lines and link computer networks to telephone networks.

[14] Crandall (1991).

[15] For a standard treatment of the subject that is widely applied in academic, business, and policy settings, see Porter (1980).

For example, the development of information-based mass marketing techniques makes it possible to selectively target consumers who are most likely to buy particular types of financial products and services. These marketing innovations permit new entrants to aggressively pursue traditional commercial bank customers. Moreover, the development of large credit databases and sophisticated credit-scoring techniques diminish the value of specific knowledge, reduce the importance of personal banking relationships, and make it easier to sell products outside a local market. Improvements in information processing technology facilitate the development of financial engineering and new financial service products and services, as well as make it possible to realize economies in back office and front office processing activities. While some of these developments have given banks greater flexibility in their operations, they have cost banks market power by lowering the cost of access to financial markets, facilitating the development of bank-like products, and opening U.S. markets to global competition by making it easier to transfer and process information. In addition, financial service providers outside the commercial banking industry enjoy cost advantages such as lighter regulatory or tax burdens.[16]

The effects of changes in competition in commercial banking are reflected in changes in the structure, conduct, and performance of the industry.

Structure

Compared to the banking industry in other advanced economies, the U.S. banking industry is very diverse, highly fragmented, and subject to far greater restrictions on powers. Of the 8,315 banks operating in the U.S. as of December 31, 2000, 58% had less than $100 million in assets; 37% had $100 million but less than $1 billion; 4% had $1–10 billion in assets; 1% had more than $10 billion in assets.[17] There were 665 banks operating in the Northeast with $2.18 trillion in assets; 1,425 banks in the Southeast with $1.61 trillion; 1,791 banks in the Central U.S. with $1.07 trillion; 2,144 banks in the Midwest with $419 billion; 1,384 banks in the Southwest with $302 billion; and 906 banks in the West with $654 billion.[18] One hundred sixty two of these banks were U.S. offices of foreign banks, which together controlled 20% of commercial banking assets at the end of 2000.[19] Nevertheless, the U.S. commercial banking industry was once even more diverse than it is today.

Over the period 1980–1998, there were over 8,000 mergers and acquisitions in commercial banking involving $2.4 trillion in assets. Rhoades (2000) finds that as

---

[16] The costs of banking regulation are estimated to be substantial, averaging 12-13% of non-interest income. On this basis, in 1991, when most studies of the cost of regulation in banking were conducted as well as a great deal of the debate on banking reform, the cost was $15.7billon. For an overview of cost studies, see Elliehausen (1998).

[17] Author's estimate based on data reported in the U.S. Census Bureau (2001), Section 25, No. 1177.

[18] Biggar (2001).

[19] Author's estimate based on FDIC (2002).

the industry consolidated, concentration increased at national and state market levels while remaining stable at local market levels where concentration has always been high. The share of domestic commercial banking deposits held by the largest ten U.S. banks increased from 19% in 1980 to 37% in 1998. Over the same period, the share of the largest 100 U.S. banks increased from 47% to 71%. At local market levels, Rhoades finds that the share of the three largest firms remained stable at about 67% in Metropolitan Statistical Areas, and 89% in Non-metropolitan Statistical Areas. At the end of 2000, 395 banks had assets over $1 billion and together controlled 84% of all commercial banking assets.[20] Consolidation is expected to continue in the first decade of the 21st century.[21]

While relative price changes encouraged consolidation and concentration in commercial banking, they also had the effect of lowering entry barriers and creating incentives for new entries that either competed directly in commercial bank markets or indirectly, by offering close substitutes for traditional bank products and services. Over the period 1960–2000, commercial banks' share of total financial intermediary assets fell from about 41% to 20%, while the share of assets controlled by other financial intermediaries increased from about 59% to 80%.[22]

Some of the changes in competition in financial services reflect a shift to investment oriented assets consistent with changing population demographics and a need to finance the retirement of the baby boom, however, other changes reflect a more direct competitive threat to traditional banking firms. For example, over the period 1960–2000, foreign banks entered U.S. financial services markets and competed directly against U.S. commercial banks, increasing their share of total commercial banking assets from 3.8% in 1973 to 19.9% in 2000.[23] Berger, Kashyap, and Scalise (1995) estimate that over the period 1979–1994, foreign banks won an estimated 48% of the total bank non-farm, non-financial corporate loans and increased their share of profitable C&I loans from 5.6% to 13.4%.

An equally important form of competition came from "non-bank banks." Until 1987, a loophole in the Bank Holding Company Act permitted companies outside the financial services industry to form a bank holding company and enter the banking business by creating a non-bank entity or affiliating with a bank and offering financial products and services identical to those that are offered by many commercial banks. If a firm was primarily engaged in a business other than banking, it was not regulated like a bank, which provided a significant competitive advantage: a non-bank bank could offer many of the same products and services that a commercial bank offers, yet it did not bear the cost of being regulated like a bank and was not subject to the same restrictions on powers. However, it could be chartered like a bank and it could qualify for FDIC insurance.

---

[20] Biggar (2001).

[21] For a comprehensive review of the evidence and the implications of consolidation in the financial services industry, see Berger, Demsetz, and Strahan (1998), as well as Rhoades (1994, 2000).

[22] Author's estimates based on Flow of Funds Accounts data published by the Board of Governors of the Federal Reserve.

[23] Author's estimates based on foreign bank statistics published by the Board of Governors of the Federal Reserve.

Recognizing the growth opportunities associated with providing financial services to their customers and employees, more than 200 large companies such as AT&T, Ford Motor Company, General Electric, and Sears established non-bank banks between the late 1970s and 1987. These firms compete directly in banking markets by acquiring banks and thrifts or forming credit unions and providing financial services through these affiliates. They compete indirectly in banking markets by permitting employees to invest retirement savings in company stock, enabling employees to put money into a mutual fund that allows check-writing, permitting employees to borrow funds from their retirement savings accounts, creating fixed income funds, and so on.

A 1981 Citicorp report submitted to the House Banking Committee hearings on interstate banking in April, 1985, documents the competitive threat as felt by one of the top ten banks in the U.S.[24] The report provides evidence of widespread competition from non-banks in traditional bank product service areas including deposit-taking, money market, check writing, lending, mortgage, and credit card activities. The report also provides evidence that non-bank competitors were actively engaged in a wide-range of related financial activities that were off-limits for banks including securities, insurance, real estate management, and cash management activities. Despite the banking industry's success in amending the Bank Holding Company Act to close this loophole, existing non-bank banks won exemption from the amendment and continued to eat away at the market share of commercial banks.

In summary, while the ownership of commercial banking was becoming increasingly concentrated over the period 1960–2000, the boundaries between its activities and those of other financial services were disappearing, reconfiguring the competitive playing field and creating new sources of competition. Commercial banks became just one type of firm in an increasingly fragmented financial services industry. However, unlike their competitors outside the commercial banking segment, they faced a peculiar structural conundrum: they could significantly affect the money supply and credit allocation in the economy and operated under protective regulation, yet this regulation could not protect them as the economic environment changed. Moreover, regulation restricted their ability to respond to competitive challenges wrought by these changes. The remaining sections of this chapter analyze the economic implications of the industry's predicament.

Conduct

In addition to structural change, there are a number of other indications of changing patterns of interaction in the financial services industry over the period 1960–2000. While the industry, including the commercial banking segment, grew significantly over this period, the data suggest that in relative terms, the core businesses of commercial banking – deposit taking and lending – deteriorated after 1980. Over the period 1980–2000, the nominal and proportional value of assets held by all

---

[24] See U.S. Government April 24 and 25, 1985.

financial intermediaries increased from over $4 trillion, an amount equivalent to 31% of all financial assets, to over $33 trillion or 37% of all financial assets. Thanks to the very large overall growth of financial markets, the value of commercial banking assets increased from over $1 trillion to over $6 trillion in the same period, however, the proportion of intermediary assets held by commercial banks fell from 34% to 20%. This loss of market share suggests that bank customers were abandoning traditional banking relationships in favor of substitute products and services, a shift that was stimulated by volatility in the price of money and facilitated by advances in information processing. In particular, the evidence suggests that traditional commercial bank depositors and borrowers were conducting a greater share of their financial transactions either through other financial intermediaries or directly in capital markets (disintermediation).

Two strong indicators of changing patterns of interaction in the financial services markets are trends in the volume of commercial bank deposits and loans. Over the period 1960–2000, the annual growth rate of the volume of deposits declined, particularly after 1974. The trend in borrowing is even more pronounced. The annual growth rate of the volume of loans and leases sharply declined over the same period, particularly after 1978. Figures 4.2 and 4.3, which fit linear trend lines to annual change data, show these trends graphically. Note in particular that the average annual

Table 4.1. Financial Assets by Holder Sector

Sectors	1980	%	2000	%
All Sectors	14,091	100.0	89,128	100.0
All Financial Intermediary Assets[a]	4,366	31.0	32,591	36.6
Commercial Banking Assets	1,482	33.9	6,456	19.8
Non-bank Financial Assets:	2,884	66.1	26,135	80.2
Money Market Funds	76	1.7	1,812	5.6
Mutual Funds	62	1.4	4,433	13.6
Securities Brokers/Dealers	45	1.0	1,213	3.7
Real Estate Investment Trusts	3	0.1	64	0.2
Closed-end Funds	8	0.2	167	0.5
Pension Funds (public and private)	710	16.3	7,674	23.5
Funding Corporations	16	0.4	1,127	3.5
Asset-backed Securities Issuers	–	–	1,831	5.6
Finance Companies	197	4.5	1,101	3.4
Savings Institutions	792	18.1	1,219	3.7
Credit Unions	68	1.6	442	1.4
Life Insurance	646	14.8	3,134	9.6
Other Insurance	182	4.2	870	2.7
Bank Personal Trusts	245	5.6	1,012	3.1

[a] Sum of assets in commercial banking and non-bank finance sectors.
Source: U.S. Census Bureau, Statistical Abstract of the United States: 2001. Section 25, No. 1163 (Billions of dollars as of December 31).

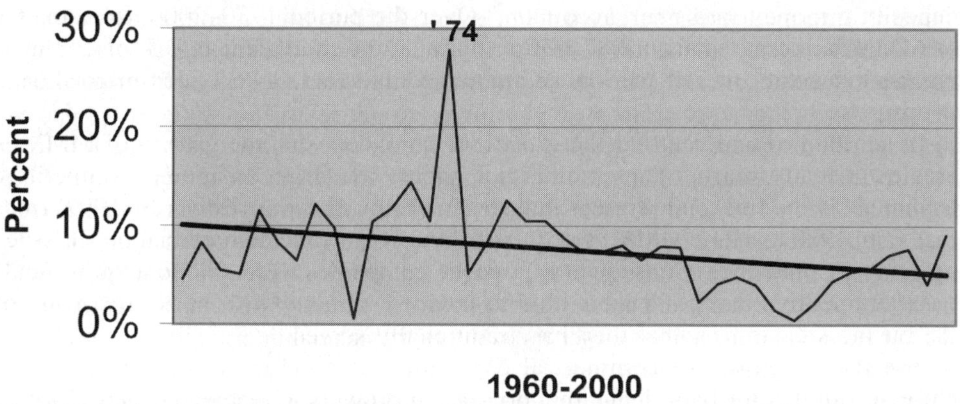

Figure 4.2. Annual Change in the Volume of Deposits.

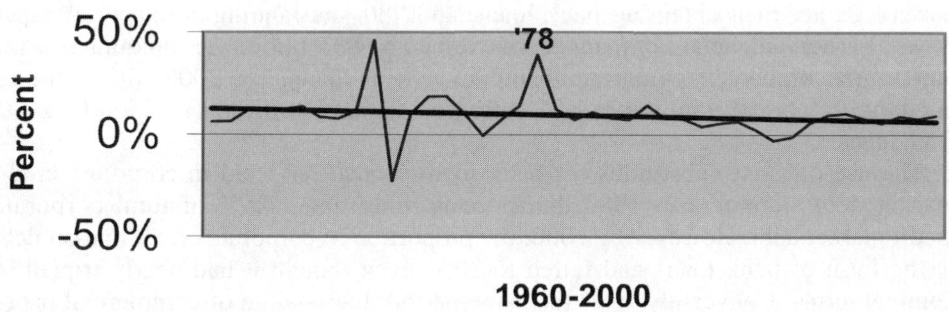

Figure 4.3. Annual Change in the Volume of Loans and Leases.

Sources for Figures 4.2 and 4.3: Author's estimate based on FDIC (2002). Figures reported compare the total for one year with the previous year.

change of both deposits and loans and leases is fairly consistently declining after 1978.[25]

Two interrelated trends further illustrate changes in conduct in the financial services industry after 1980: the growth of deposits into Money Market Mutual Funds (MMMFs) and the growth of commercial paper. Both trends were driven by innovations in the securities industry in response to changes in the relative price of money and information processing. MMMFs, which provide a means for investors with limited financial resources to park cash safely for a short period of time and reap relatively high short-term interest rates, are a close substitute for

[25] Berger, Kashyap and Scalise (1995) decompose this change for the period 1979–1994, finding that U.S. commercial banks' share of the total credit market debt fell from 25.8% in 1979 to 17% in 1994, their share of non-credit market debt fell from 22.6% to 14.4%, and their share of non-farm, non-financial corporate debt fell from 19.6% to 14.5%

depositing money into bank accounts.[26] Over the period 1980–2000, investments in MMMFs increased from $77 billion, an amount equivalent to 5% of commercial bank deposits, to $1.8 trillion, an amount equivalent to 44% of commercial bank deposits.[27]

In addition to undercutting the growth of bank deposits, the growth of MMMFs created a ready market for commercial paper, which reconfigured competitive advantage in the financial services industry in yet another way. Edwards (1997) finds that from 1980 to 1994, MMMFs acquired about 60% of the commercial paper issued by finance companies. Consequently, finance companies were able to acquire funds on a competitive basis and were able to compete directly with banks for many of the business customers that they had traditionally served.

The rate of growth of commercial paper illustrates the trend toward the use of close substitutes for bank loans by corporate borrowers. Commercial paper, which consists of short-term, unsecured promissory notes issued primarily by corporations, is a financial instrument that permits companies to raise short-term funds in capital markets rather than obtaining bank loans. In 1980, outstanding commercial paper issued by non-financial companies was valued at $37 billion, an amount equivalent to 9% of banks' commercial and industrial loans. By 2000, the value of outstanding commercial paper had increased to $343 billion, or 33% of banks' C&I loans.[28]

The use of close substitutes for bank loans is also reflected in corporate credit market debt statistics. In 1980, bank loans represented 25% of total corporate credit market debt. However by 2000, the proportion of corporate credit market debt in the form of bank loans had fallen to 20%, even though it had nearly tripled in nominal terms. Conversely, over the same period, the volume of commercial paper and corporate bonds increased from 3% to 6% and from 40% to 47% respectively.

In summary, patterns of interaction in the financial services industry over the period 1960–2000, indicate that there were significant changes in the competitive landscape of commercial banking, particularly after 1980. Despite overall growth in the financial services industry and the commercial banking segment of this industry, commercial banks lost market share in their core businesses. Their ability to respond to competition by diversifying either geographically or through product and service offerings was constrained by regulation. Regulatory constraints on diver-

---

[26] A mutual fund is an open-end investment company that pools money invested by shareholders and invests these funds in a variety of securities including stocks, bonds, and money market instruments. They provide liquidity to investors by standing ready to buy back shares at current net asset value. The funds, which may be taxable or tax-exempt, specialize in investing in low-risk short-term securities such as bonds and commercial paper with maturities of 30–180 days. Mutual fund companies are governed by a Board of Directors and managed by a professional management team. They do not have federal deposit guarantees and are regulated by the Securities and Exchange Commission under the Investment Company Act of 1940.

[27] Author's estimate. Data sources for mutual funds are U.S. Census Bureau (2001), Section 25, No. 1214, and FDIC (2002) for the value of deposits.

[28] Author's estimate. Data sources for commercial paper are U.S. Census Bureau (2001), Section 25, No. 1197, and FDIC (2002) for the value of C&I loans.

Table 4.2. Corporate Credit Market Debt

Instrument	1980	%	2000	%
All Corporate Credit Market Debt	907	100.0	4,741	100.0
Commercial Paper	28	3.1	278	5.9
Corporate Bonds	366	40.4	2,234	47.1
Bank Loans	230	25.4	926	19.5
Other Loans and Advances:	110	12.1	692	14.6
Savings Institutions	1	0.1	20	0.4
Finance Companies	78	8.6	424	8.9
U.S. Government	8	0.9	7	0.1
Acceptance Liabilities to Banks	17	1.9	4	0.1
Rest of the World	5	0.6	120	2.5
Asset-based Securities Issuers	–	–	116	2.4
All Other	173	19.1	611	12.9

Source: U.S. Census Bureau, Statistical Abstract of the United States: 2001. Section 25, No. 1165 (Billions of dollars as of December 31).

sification, which are discussed in detail in Chapter Five, forced banks to focus on institutional change and to find new ways to compete in core business segments. The significance of these restrictions is suggested by statistics on economic performance, to which we now turn.

Performance

The impact of changes in structure and conduct is further reflected in the financial performance of the commercial banking industry. While total bank income increased over the period 1960–2000, the annual rate of growth declined. Income growth was particularly weak in the 1960s, 1980s, and 1990s.[29] Looking at return on total assets (ROTA), which is a comprehensive measure of bank profitability, profitability appears to hold up rather well: ROTA is increasing over the period 1960–2000 to well over 1.0%. However, for most of the period 1970–1990, ROTA is at or below 1.0%.[30] Slow growth and weak returns create pressure to improve performance that a business manager in a publicly held firm cannot ignore.

The impact of regulatory restraints on diversification is suggested by non-interest income statistics. Non-interest income, which includes service charges and fees, income from fiduciary activities, gains, losses, and fees from foreign currency or exchange transactions, futures and forward contracts, asset management, or the sale or disposition of loans, premises, and fixed assets, and other miscellaneous income, provides a more stable source of income than interest income and also

[29] See data appendix (A2) for detail.

[30] ROTA is calculated by dividing a bank's net income by its total average assets during a given period. Historically, most banks have ROTAs within a range of 60%–1.5%. See data appendix (A3) for detail.

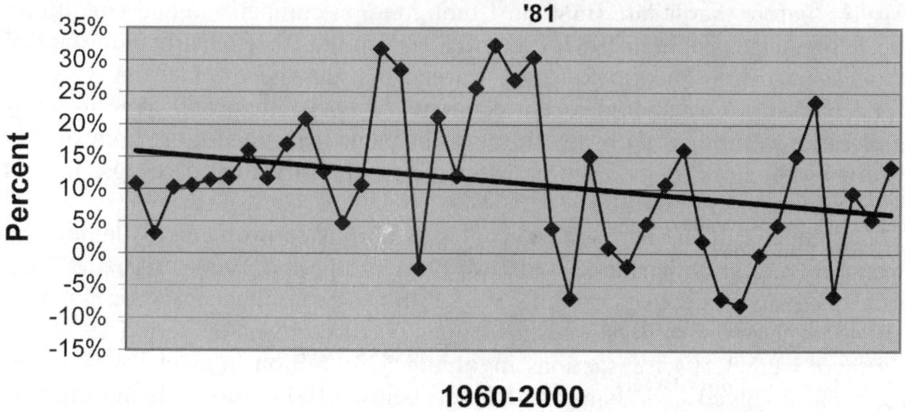

Figure 4.4. Annual Change in Total Income.

Source: Author's estimate based on FDIC (2002). Also see data appendix (A2).

indicates the extent to which banks have diversified away from core bank products and services.[31] In 1960, non-interest income represented 15% of total income however it consistently declines after 1960, reaching a low of 7% in 1981. After 1981, non-interest income begins to increase but does not reach 15% until 1990. After 1990, it steadily increases to a new high of 34% in 1996, indicating that commercial bank managers are making progress finding new sources of income outside of core business segments.

While income and return on investment were deteriorating, the commercial banking industry's net interest margin (NIM) improved after 1974, suggesting that bank managers did a fairly good job of managing assets and liabilities in the face of competitive pressures. NIM was consistently above 3% over the period 1960–2000 and reached a high of 4.4% in 1992. However, industry capital ratios, which reflect changes in profitability and risk, were on a downward trend, falling from 8% in 1960 to a worrisome low of 5.7% in 1974 and 1979.[32] They remained relatively low for much of the 1980s, increasing to just 6.2% in 1989.[33] The implementation of risk-based capital standards in 1988 (the Basle Accord) coincides with an improvement in capital ratios however it was not until 1992 that they returned to healthy levels.

[31] Interest income, which is all income earned on interest-bearing assets, is derived from the core business segments of banking, e.g. making loans and managing assets.

[32] The capital ratio is the ratio of total equity capital to total assets. In general, the higher the capital ratio, the more conservatively a bank is managed. A high capital ratio also indicates the ability to grow. Failure to meet capital guidelines can subject a bank to a variety of enforcement actions, including termination of deposit insurance and restrictions on business activities.

[33] Before 1981, capital regulation was relatively discretionary. New flat rate standards implemented in the early 1980s created incentives for banks to adjust their portfolio risks to meet standards. It is generally argued that many banks increased their credit risk exposure during the 1980s (see for example Boyd and Gertler, 1993 and Berger, Kashyap, and Scalise, 1995).

Testifying before the Senate Banking Committee on competition and conditions in the U.S. financial system in 1981, Frederick H. Schultz, Vice Chairman of the Board of Governors of the Federal Reserve, warned that despite the fact that U.S. commercial banks had weathered recent economic events rather well, deterioration in capital ratios combined with deterioration in bank loan portfolios, both of which are better indicators of medium and long-term viability than earnings, indicated serious problems in the industry.[34]

The acuteness of the banking industry's performance problems is demonstrated by bank closing and assistance statistics. Over the period 1960–1992, 1,697 commercial banks with deposits totaling $247 billion were either closed or assisted by the FDIC. The majority of these transactions occurred over the period 1979–1992, when there were 1,504 transactions involving $230 billion in assets: 84% of these transactions involved small banks with assets below $100 million, which were poorly positioned to meet the challenges wrought by economic change and competitive dynamics.[35]

In short, the performance of commercial banks deteriorated for much of the period 1980–1992, when competitive shocks began to take their toll. The annual change in commercial bank income slowed and returns weakened. While bank managers maintained healthy net interest margins, they allowed capital ratios to fall below 7%, which increased systemic risk. The magnitude of this risk is evident in closing and assistance statistics, which reflect the effects of a full-blown banking crisis in the 1980s and early 1990s.

Summary

Competition in commercial banking significantly changed over the period 1960–2000. A number of domestic and international forces stimulated change in the economic environment of commercial banking. Changes in the prices of money and information processing combined with rapid growth in demand for financial services led to new competition and the creation of close substitutes for core banking services with better price-performance trade-offs. Competitive shocks eroded the traditional boundaries between banking and securities markets, created new opportunities for non-bank banks, and reconfigured structure and conduct in commercial banking and financial services. However, regulatory restraints on powers limited banks' ability to respond to competitive opportunities and threats and economic performance suffered, particularly over the period 1980–1992.

Economic change in the financial services industry ended the quiet life of bankers and bank regulators. The problem posed by change was to survive in a rapidly

---

[34] U.S. Government, April 18, May 6, 7, 1981. The events Schultz referred to were interest rate volatility (the prime rate rose from 13.25% to almost 20%, fell to 11% and then rose again to 21.5%), a program of credit restraint, a short recession, unabated inflation, and federal deregulation of various activities of deposit-taking institutions.

[35] Author's estimates based on FDIC (2002).

changing industry and defend market share in competition with lower cost firms that were technically more sophisticated and faced fewer constraints on powers. Because of the changing nature of demand for financial services, restrictions on diversification through geographic expansion or product and service offerings were particularly onerous. Competitiveness, and indeed survival, required implementing new strategies to improve risk-return trade-offs. Economic change required institutional change in private and public sectors, including reorganization of banks and regulatory relief from restraints on powers. The key to understanding the capacity of a regulated industry to respond to competitive shocks is determining the extent to which institutional arrangements permit firms to both respond to threats and pursue new opportunities. The analysis continues in Chapter Five, which examines institutional change over the period 1960–2000.

CHAPTER FIVE

Institutional Change 1960–2000

Other studies of institutional change in U.S. banking have focused on legislative and regulatory change. Certainly these processes are important aspects of institutional change however, they are not sufficient proxies. Institutions are the "rules of the game" that solve collective action problems in a particular setting by governing interaction, outcomes, and information flows.[1] They reflect the beliefs and preferences of those who design them and they shape the beliefs and preferences of those who follow them. As in other regulated industries in the United States, banking institutions exist in the public and private sectors and are quite diverse, encompassing norms, laws, regulations, contracts, charters, bylaws, policies, standard operating procedures, and so on. In *toto*, institutions reduce uncertainty by creating incentives to act (or not) and imposing constraints on the range of feasible activities in a particular situation.

The analysis in this chapter focuses on the types of institutional change that occurred in U.S. commercial banking over the period 1960–2000, and the processes associated with these changes. Section One describes the evolution of commercial banking institutions and analyzes policy design issues. Section Two analyzes institutional change in the private and public sectors over the period 1960–2000, and Section Three summarizes and concludes.

Background

The institutions that today govern U.S. commercial banking activities are a product of the structure of the U.S. political economy, which favors local control, and a solution to the collective action problems that are inherent to growth and development in an economy that is very large, quite diverse, and both decentralized and polycentric. A bank, as distinct from other types of financial services enterprises, is defined to mean any institution that both accepts demand deposits and

[1] "Institution" has been defined as a rule or set of rules that permits, requires, or prohibits a set of actions in a specific situation (E. Ostrom, 1986; North, 1993). An organization is a set of rules that structures purposeful activity. For a detailed discussion of concepts related to institutional analysis and design, see Polski and Ostrom (1999).

is engaged in the business of making commercial loans. In addition to complying with state and federal business and commercial laws, the owner(s) of a U.S. commercial bank, which may stand-alone or be owned by a Bank Holding Company (BHC), must obtain a charter from either the state in which it is incorporated or the federal government. This "dual banking system" of state and nationally chartered banks has produced three primary federal regulatory agencies and fifty state agencies, which are involved in chartering, monitoring, and enforcing rules that govern structure, balance sheet composition, business activities, and pricing.[2] The Board of Governors of the Federal Reserve, the Office of the Comptroller of the Currency (OCC) and the Federal Deposit Insurance Corporation (FDIC) regulate banks with national charters. State supervisory commissions regulate state chartered banks that are not insured by the FDIC, insured banks that are not members of the Federal Reserve System (non-member banks), and state banks that are members of the Federal Reserve System (member banks). State-chartered banks are subject to Federal oversight if they are members of the Federal Reserve System or if the FDIC insures them. The Federal Reserve supervises some activities of uninsured state banks, such as mergers and acquisitions, as well as the activities of BHCs, and Financial Holding Companies (FHCs).[3] The FDIC cooperates with the OCC and state regulatory authorities to supervise all insured banks. Effectively, most commercial banks are regulated by the Federal Reserve: as of December 31, 2000, 79% of all commercial banks were affiliated with BHCs, and BHCs controlled 93% of all commercial bank assets.[4]

U.S. banking institutions were not cut from whole cloth but evolved along with the structure of political authority and economic development in the United States. The polycentric structure of control of money and banking originates in colonial America. England's nineteen North American colonies, which extended from Florida to Newfoundland and were separately chartered, had very different finance needs and equally idiosyncratic monetary systems. However, they had a common and chronic shortage of hard currency, which stimulated the demand for money and credit. This demand was met by issuing paper money through private credit associations and colonial governments. In many instances, private and public bills of credit circulated as legal tender, creating a very fragmented monetary system that generated high rates of inflation and frequent litigation over the value of contractual obligations.

---

[2] Note that if a Bank Holding Company is engaged in insurance or securities activities, it is also subject to regulation by governing authorities in these financial services segments.

[3] The Graham Leach Bliley Act of 1999 removes restrictions on powers for BHCs and foreign banks that meet conditions to be deemed a Financial Holding Company (FHC). The Act streamlines supervision for all BHCs including those that operate as FHCs and specifies the relationship between the Federal Reserve and other regulators.

[4] As of December 31, 2000, 6,519 commercial banks were affiliated with BHCs: 41% of affiliated banks were members of the Federal Reserve and 68% of member banks had national bank charters. Author's calculation based upon data reported in the Federal Reserve Board Annual Report 2000.

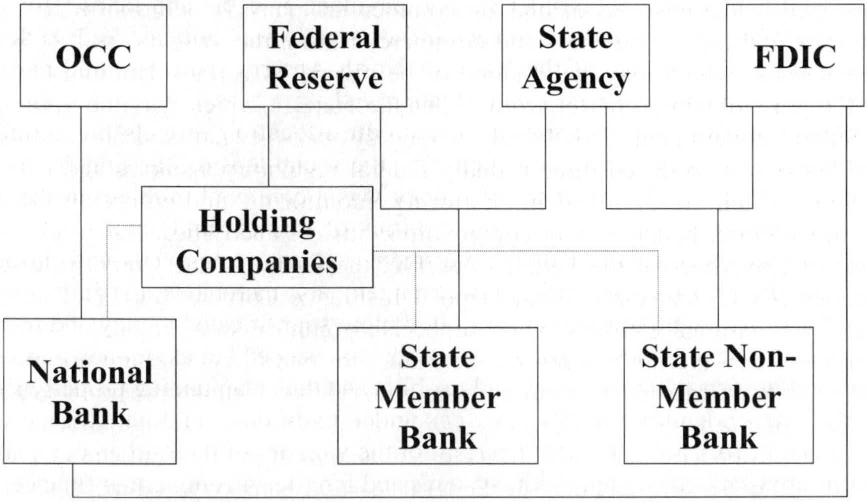

Figure 5.1. Commercial Banking Oversight.

Trade between England and her colonies exposed the members of the system to each other's monetary and commercial policies, which generated increasing instability in the English commercial system.[5] In response, Parliament limited monetary freedom in 1741 by extending the Bubble Act of 1720 to the colonies, which suppressed the development of private banking associations. Subsequent acts of Parliament further restricted colonial monetary activities. In addition to limiting the development of commercial banking, these restrictions (among other policy insults – most notably tax policies) led to the Declaration of Independence and war for independence.

To help finance the war for independence, private subscribers in Philadelphia formed the Bank of North America under a limited charter issued by the Continental Congress. As the first publicly chartered money-bank in America, it led the way for the development of commercial banking. However, the war left the republic with limited trading opportunities, high unemployment, deeply in debt, repeatedly beset by severe financial crises, in sore need of economic stimulation, and with no central coordinating authority to facilitate commerce and trade. The value of state and continental paper money issues plummeted to zero, arousing deep suspicion against any enterprise, private or public, that engaged in banking and issued paper money. Issues pertaining to money and banking generated not only intense and prolonged public debate but more seriously for the stability of the nascent republic,

[5] Prices varied from colony to colony and debtors were legally shielded from outside creditors by the right to pay in money with a face value less than that of their debt (Hammond, 1957). The effects of perverse commercial institutions and poor economic management in some of the colonies were thus transmitted among trading partners.

frequent uprisings and rebellions over the payment of debts and taxes. However, the gap between the demand for money and its supply was critical. And so despite public clamor, the charter of the Bank of North America was renewed and new bank charter applications were liberally approved.[6]

Political controversy over money and credit allocation reflects the economic circumstances of early Americans, including the social tensions arising from commercial development. The scarcity of money was a continual problem in the early American economy. While close communities of farmers and small-scale farm-related businesses could meet their investment and operating needs with informal barter and short-term reciprocal credit arrangements, merchants and industrialists engaged in arms-length transactions required more sophisticated money and banking arrangements. Nevertheless, agricultural producers needed banks: money and credit were essential for paying mortgage and tax bills and thus maintaining property rights. Fiercely independent and able to prosper under traditional land-banking arrangements, country folk had little appreciation for the vagaries of their urban compatriots need for large-scale merchant credit systems and long-term commercial finance. The strict enforcement of debt payment terms that was so critical to establishing a credible and reliable commercial system based upon impersonal exchange over long distances, imposed a new and arguably unnecessary strain on rural economic relations, where transactions were personalized and localized. As commercial lending institutions spilled over into agricultural lending, tensions developed that fueled political efforts to constrain the development of a central banking system.

While early American policymakers debated how best to manage the new nation's debt and organize the banking system, the need for funds to develop the economy and fight wars persisted. Responding to this need, state authorities liberally approved new bank charters, which resulted in a large, uncoordinated industry composed of local banking monopolies. The fragmented structure of the early American banking industry created a number of costly coordination problems. First, independent local banks' uncoordinated note issues generated inflation and unstable currency exchange rates. In effect, each bank was a separate monetary system. The failure to coordinate among these separate systems created monetary instability and led to frequent currency depreciations and financial crises. The absence of a sound currency fueled speculation, exacerbated business cycle effects, undermined the credibility of public credit at home and abroad, and inhibited sustained growth and development.

A second coordination problem was the absence of an inexpensive, equitable, and reliable payment system in which the notes of domestic and foreign banks could be redeemed at a value that was as close to real par value as possible. As economic activity expanded beyond local communities, country money piled up in money-center banks in the cities on a regular basis. Money-center banks – if they agreed to redeem country bank notes – only did so at a discount. Adding insult to injury, country banks were forced to settle with the money-center banks in specie, which

---

[6] By 1836, 713 banks had been chartered and had deposits totaling $166 million (Hixson, 1993).

eroded their capital base and lending capacity, threatened their safety and soundness, and further fueled regional political-economic tensions.[7]

A third coordination problem was related to unmet short-term liquidity constraints. Recall the description of the nature of the banking business in Chapter Four. In a fractional reserve system when transaction requirements exceed reserves a bank faces a short-term liquidity constraint. With no short-term lending facility, assets must be sold to meet transaction demands. Premature asset liquidation imposes a cost (in the form of investment losses) that can push a bank into insolvency. With no lender of last resort, an insolvent bank fails and bank creditors incur losses. In a ripple-like effect, creditors' losses then constrain their ability to meet their other financial obligations and to capitalize on investment opportunities. When credit tightens, the economy contracts. In this way, quite independent of economic fundamentals, bank failures can undermine the smooth functioning of a financial system, as well as confidence in its ability to meet economic needs.

The first three coordination failures in the early American banking system combined to create a fourth type of coordination problem: the need to protect bank creditors from bank failures. The chronic failure to coordinate to control inflation increased lending risk. The absence of a short-term lending facility and a reliable payment system impaired safe asset transformation, particularly in the presence of currency instability. On top of these inadequacies, banks were poorly managed. Small banks were particularly renowned for their poor management practices.[8] Absent generally accepted accounting principles, informative financial disclosures, financially sophisticated consumers, and prudential supervision, it was impossible for depositors and borrowers to assess the quality of individual banks. With limited information and knowledge and in the presence of monopoly chartering, there was no consistently effective means to discipline banking activities.

Finally, the slow growth of theoretical and practical knowledge of monetary policy, economic management, and business management conspired against sound banking. Scholars, bankers, policy makers, and consumers alike were learning as their economies developed and integrated. Economic historians have documented a consistent and pervasive failure in the 18th and 19th centuries to understand the political and economic implications of money and banking activities in America.[9]

---

[7] Hammond (1957) argues that in the first 60 years of American banking, rival banks regardless of geographic location, routinely and "rapaciously" raided one another thusly: a loan by one bank (Bank 1) placed a competitor bank (Bank 2) in possession of claims against it. These claims enabled Bank 2 to make demands upon the reserves of Bank 1, thereby reducing the lending capacity of Bank 1 and competition for loans for Bank 2.

[8] This phenomenon persists in the 21st century. Looking at selected measures of financial condition based on asset size, the smallest commercial banks (less than $100 million in assets) are more likely to lose money than larger banks and financial returns (as measured by return on assets and return on equity) are lower. See U.S. Census Bureau, Statistical Abstract of the United States: 2000, Table 1177. Small banks also failed at a higher rate than large banks during the banking crises of 1980s and early 1990s.

[9] See for example, Hammond (1957), Hixson (1993), Kindleberger (1996[1978]), and Redlich (1968).

Geographically dispersed and with little coordination across local networks, Americans had limited exposure to the experience of others. This meant that knowledge of sound money and banking practices developed slowly and was transmitted haphazardly.

As the effects of these coordination problems made them selves felt, a number of institutional solutions were launched. These solutions took three forms: hierarchical coordination, market coordination, and mixed systems of coordination. Hierarchical coordination, which may be centralized or decentralized, relies upon a single source of controlling authority and thus regulation has an involuntary aspect. By contrast, regulation based upon market coordination, which has many overlapping centers of authority, is purely voluntary. Mixed coordination systems rely on a combination of hierarchical and market coordination mechanisms, and voluntary and involuntary control.[10]

Coordination in the early American banking system evolved from a hierarchical to a mixed system of coordination. During colonial times, England formally retained the authority to regulate money and banking on a centralized basis. Initially, she permitted the colonial states to coordinate and regulate these affairs, effectively decentralizing banking regulation. However, there were few rules and oversight and supervision were sparse so the system defaulted to market-based coordination with voluntary regulation. When coordination problems emerged that threatened her interests, England attempted to regulate on a centralized basis. However, distance and the primitive nature of information technology made centralized regulatory control quite difficult in practice.

Markets continued to function as the primary means of coordination in the colonies until the war for independence created the need to coordinate more closely in order to achieve political objectives. During the war years, the Continental Congress, with the agreement of the states, exercised primary control over money and banking through the Bank of North America. After the war, the states reasserted their control but exercised their authority on a *lassiez faire* basis, and the system again defaulted to market-based coordination.

Wishing to promote rapid American economic development after the war by organizing capital to invest on a large scale in trade and manufacturing capacity, Hamilton promoted a national regulatory scheme for monetary affairs that would control the money supply, regulate inflation, and standardize commercial transactions. Conceived as one very special money-bank among many, the First National Bank was designed to exercise monetary control by operating with large capital facilitated by centralizing the deposit of government funds, permitting it to make other (state-chartered) banks its debtors, promulgating conservative banking policies, and cooperating with the U.S. Treasury. Influenced by the writings of Adam Smith and actively involved in designing both a national banking charter and state banking

[10] In addition to banking, another good contemporary example of mixed coordination in U.S. financial services is the regulation of securities exchange activities. Privately organized exchanges promulgate rules and monitor and discipline their members subject to supervision by the federal Securities and Exchange Commission.

charters, Hamilton did not seek a national monopoly on the provision of banking services. Instead, he sought a stable currency by means of centralized control, exercised by a privately owned banking firm bound by public charter to serve national interests rather than particular or local interests.

Eschewing large-scale commercial development, debt-finance, money-banking and, in particular, the monopoly of a national bank as an "evil," Jefferson argued that a national bank "might swallow up the others and monopolize the whole banking business of the U.S."[11] Instead, he favored a system of state-chartered local banks in which government deposits were spread out among banks owned by the people, rather than in a single, national bank. By opposing centralized credit allocation, Jefferson hoped to protect local political and economic interests against domination by large commercial enterprises. The anticipated advantage of this demand-driven, market-oriented development model was to permit an agricultural sector organized on the basis of small-scale enterprise owned and managed by independent "Freemen" to thrive-a-pace with commercial and industrial sectors organized on a larger scale by more affluent citizens.

Estimating that citizens' preferences for centralized monetary control were dangerously unstable and that this instability could destroy the fragile consensus that supported the new republic, Madison also opposed a national bank. Others, like Adams, just didn't like the banking business.[12] Some misunderstood the nature of banking and the relationship between responsible financial intermediation and irresponsible speculation.[13] Others were morally opposed to debt finance. Nevertheless, the benefit to the national treasury and the republican cause of centralizing the issue of legal tender at the federal government level was not lost on even the most ardent advocate of states' rights and individual liberty: Jefferson and Hamilton both supported this constitutional proposal. Moreover, despite his rhetoric against debt finance and the banking business, Jefferson was quite willing to charter banks to serve his political interests.[14]

---

[11] Jefferson to Gallatin as cited by Redlich (1968, p. 21). Jefferson was the chief spokesman for the developing theory of local government based on the ideas of the radical agrarians, whose opposition to national banking, the "aristocracy of credit," and a paper money system was articulated by John Taylor, Philip Freneau, and a half-generation later by Andrew Jackson. This group believed that "paper men," who represented the interests of banks, sought election to Congress where they could further private interests at the expense of public interest. In the view of the radical agrarians, bankers' interest in large government deposits, which could only be had from taxes, created incentives for legislators to pursue high tax policies.

[12] Adams' view on banking is expressed in a letter to Taylor, 12 March 1819, as cited by Hixson (1993): "I have never had but one opinion of banking . . . and that opinion has uniformly been that the banks have done more injury to the religion, morality, tranquility, property, and even the wealth of the nation, than they have done or ever will do good. They are a delusion of the many for the interest of the few."

[13] To be sure, given the dearth of knowledge and institutional constraints, there was often more of the later than the former in early American financial history.

[14] For detailed historical analyses of "political banks," see Hammond (1957), Hixson (1993), and Redlich (1968). Redlich argues that bank chartering became so politicized that the public became convinced that banks were only chartered as instruments of political parties and that this conviction

At the same time that policy makers were debating the virtues of national banking, coalitions of political and economic entrepreneurs launched a number of stopgap initiatives to solve coordination problems based on both market and mixed systems of coordination. Deposit insurance funds were created to protect creditors from bank failures and to create incentives for sound bank management. Most of these were organized on a private, voluntary basis. However, there were a few public-private initiatives. The New York Safety Fund, created in 1829, is one example: Michigan and Vermont adopted similar plans at around the same time. The Suffolk Bank system, which was formed in 1818 in Massachusetts, inspired the formation of voluntary associations to clear and redeem country money.

Unsurprisingly, voluntary regulation was not sufficient to cope with the pressures created by uneven economic development, westward expansion, and rapid industrial growth. Control over banking was a natural lightning rod for the rapidly developing tension between agrarian and commercial interests, country hamlets and urban cities, the hierarchical institutional designs of the Hamiltonian Federalists, and the polycentric designs of the Jeffersonian Republicans. While Congress twice granted a provisional national banking charter – the First National Bank of the U.S. was chartered from 1791–1811 and the Second National Bank of the U.S. was chartered from 1816–1832 – the institutional and economic exigencies of American life made it very difficult to build an adequate constituency for central banking and involuntary regulatory control. The politically numerous pioneers, who wanted easy money to farm and provide goods and services to agricultural communities, opposed national regulation. The First and Second National Banks lacked the full powers of a *bona fide* central bank. Hence, they were only partially successful in ameliorating the monetary coordination problems that plagued the banking system. Paradoxically, their modest success at controlling the money supply is widely cited as the cause of their downfall. In the face of tightening by the National Bank, state banks could not sustain easy money policies without risking failure. Fanning populist fears of monopoly control of credit allocation and economic resentment toward money-center banks, the state chartered banks secured Congressional support to withdraw the charter of the First National Bank and Presidential support to veto Congress' renewal of the charter of the Second National Bank.[15]

When voluntary and involuntary regulation failed, Americans deepened their

---

played a large part in the fight against the Second Bank of the U.S. (1968, pp. 22–23). And of course Jefferson's personal experience of debt finance is well established in the literature on the founders. See for example, Ellis [1996] 1998.

[15] In a cogent case of how politics make strange bedfellows, radical agrarians, land speculators, and the states had a common interest in maintaining a polycentric banking system. All three groups wanted easy money. The first group wanted to be able to pay property taxes, and the second group wanted to be able to borrow on more comfortable terms in order to finance speculative purchases from the states of lands confiscated from the British. The states wanted to be able to collect on the sales of confiscated lands and levy taxes on banks and bank financed activities. Moreover, some states also owned banks.

use of market mechanisms to coordinate money and banking activities. In the 1830's the "free banking" movement took hold of the popular imagination, fomented by the Equal Rights Party (Loco-Focus), a radical, breakaway wing of the Democratic Party. The party opposed chartering banks, arguing that in doing so, the sovereignty of the people passed from the legislature to the chartered institution, corrupting democracy and creating economic monopolies. Conceding that banking should be a free trade, states relaxed their control and passed laws that led to state banks being chartered under general rules of incorporation rather than special acts of state legislatures. The first enabling law was passed in New York in 1838. The New York model spread west in the 1840s and 1850s.

Alas, the policy triumph of markets over hierarchy resulted in persistent failures and panics in the banking system: serious domestic crises occurred in 1857, 1873, 1884, 1893, and 1907. While the heterogeneous and geographically disbursed system of independent local banks envisioned by Jefferson facilitated economic development that was responsive to the demands of local citizens on a very large scale, it achieved this at the cost of economic stability. Dubbed "wildcat" banking and absent policies and conditions that permitted true banking competition, free banking policies stimulated growth in the number of banks without increasing the quality of banking. This development only exacerbated coordination problems that worsened as the states' economies became more tightly integrated.

The enactment of the National Currency Act of 1863 and the National Bank Act of 1864, launched a new era of mixed coordination but this time in the direction of hierarchical coordination and regulated market-based competition. The banking legislation passed in the 1860s created a "dual" banking system by authorizing federally chartered banks regulated by the newly formed Office of the Comptroller of the Currency (OCC), a Special Office of the U.S. Treasury Department. A dual regulatory system permitted bank owners to choose between competing state and federal regulatory authorities, and banking consumers to select between competing national or state supervised banks. Previous attempts to regulate money and banking at the national level had failed largely because of the opposition of the states, which believed that it was in their interest to maintain local control. The dual chartering system allowed states to retain regulatory authority but forced them to compete with a national regulator.[16] This uniquely American institutional design, which employs the checks and balances of "opposite and rival interests" so beloved by Madison, incorporates incentives to protect bankers from excess regulation and to protect consumers from inadequate supervision.[17]

---

[16] By some accounts, the Currency and Bank acts represented a cleverly designed tack in the direction of federal control (White, 1986). The acts included a tax on state-chartered banks. Some hoped the dual system would eliminate state-chartered banks through a combination of regulated competition and taxation, leaving only nationally chartered banks, and hence a federally controlled banking system. However, bank owners resisted this scheme by exploiting the flexibility of the institutional design, and thereby not only survived, but they prospered.

[17] For an extensive analysis of Madison's thinking on local versus federal control, see Banning, 1995.

While the national banking acts of the 1860s addressed the problem of regulatory control of banks, it did not solve monetary coordination problems. Financial crises continued unabated and further national bank regulation was passed to create safety and soundness in the financial system. A particularly severe crisis in 1907 prompted Congress to establish the National Monetary Commission, which put forth proposals to create an institution that would manage financial disruptions. After considerable debate, a central bank was created in 1913. The Federal Reserve Act stated that its purposes were "to provide for the establishment of Federal reserve banks, to furnish an elastic currency, to afford means to rediscounting commercial paper, to establish a more effective supervision of banking in the United States, and for other purposes." Subsequent legislative action expanded and clarified the objectives of the Federal Reserve to include economic growth in line with the economy's potential to expand, a high level of employment, stable prices, and moderate long-term interest rates.[18]

Until the dual banking system was created in the 1860s, the states were the primary bank regulators in the United States. While branching was tightly controlled in order to protect local bank monopolies, powers were relatively unregulated until federal regulation in the late 1920s and 1930s: banks were free to engage in a wide range of financial services activities and determine their business policies and practices. In the late 19th century and early 20th century, there was limited pressure to engage in either intrastate branching or interstate banking in the United States due to the localized pattern of domestic commerce. The National Bank Act of 1864 prohibited nationally chartered banks from branching. For state chartered banks, branching rules varied by state. Most states were "unit banking" states that allowed a bank to operate at only one physical location. A few states allowed some branching subject to within-state geographic limitations. Only California allowed statewide branching for its banks. National banks were limited to single locations regardless of state branching rules. State and national banking rules prohibited interstate banking, except that the Edge Act of 1919 permitted banks to conduct business across state lines in competition with foreign banks.

As the domestic and international political economies integrated in the early 20th century, competition, technological change, and burgeoning commercial activity put commercial banks subject to unit banking rules at a competitive disadvantage. It is at this time that group and chain banking emerges under the umbrella of Bank Holding Companies as a means to evade these restrictions.[19] Economic integration also exposed banks to new types and levels of financial risk, which the banking system was not able to contain: the frailty of the system became painfully apparent

[18] In its 2000 Annual Report, the Federal Reserve describes its mission as follows: ". . . to foster the stability, integrity, and efficiency of the nation's monetary, financial, and payment systems so as to promote optimal macroeconomic performance." Characteristically, the U.S. "central bank" has a polycentric design. For an overview of the structure of the U.S. Federal Reserve System, see www.federalreserve.gov.

[19] See Savage (1978) for a comparison of the bank holding company movements in the early and late 20th century.

with economic crises of the late 1920s and 1930s. The loss of confidence in markets generated by the economic crises arising from the stock market crash of 1929 and the Great Depression produced a decade of reforms that tilted the balance of control toward hierarchical coordination and away from market coordination through the enactment of seven national banking statutes intended to strengthen the system. These laws formally segmented banking activities, established tight controls on activities, and created a federal deposit insurance program. In 1927, the McFadden Act was passed to permit the banking industry to restructure in response to the failure of many rural banks in the 1920s.[20] The Act prohibited interstate banking but permitted national banks to establish branches within their same city of operation if the law of that state also permitted state chartered banks to do the same. In 1933, the Banking Act (Glass Steagall) was enacted, which created the FDIC and separated commercial banking from investment banking, establishing them as separate lines of business. Two years later the Banking Act of 1935 was enacted, which established the FDIC as a permanent agency of the government.

Nevertheless, managers of financial services businesses could legally avoid some restrictions on their activities by structuring ownership under the umbrella of a holding company. However, this began to change with passage of the Bank Holding Company Act of 1956. This Act made multi-bank holding companies (MBHCs) subject to supervision by the Board of Governors of the Federal Reserve, required the approval of the Federal Reserve Board for establishing a bank holding company, and prohibited MBHCs headquartered in one state from acquiring a bank in another state. Under the Act, the Federal Reserve approves applications for *de novo* BHC formation, mergers and acquisitions involving BHCs, and the banking activities of BHCs. The merger and acquisition decisions of the Federal Reserve are subject to review by the antitrust division of the Department of Justice. While the Federal Reserve must coordinate with the FDIC and state regulatory authorities over the supervision of banks owned by BHCs, the activities of BHCs are primarily supervised by the Federal Reserve. Initially, the Act applied only to multi-bank holding companies (MBHCs): one-bank holding companies (OBHCs) were excluded.

In summary, the system of banking regulation that has evolved in the United States over the past 250 years is a polycentric hybrid that is an amalgamation of the hierarchical system favored by the Hamiltonian Federalists and the polycentric system espoused by Jeffersonian democratic Republicans. Prior to the passage of national laws, the states controlled banks, and banking regulation was largely voluntary. While economic conditions occasionally inspired banks and states to coordinate to solve the systemic problems that arose from their independent activities, just as often, competitive forces operated against coordination. Voluntary regulation could not contain the monetary instability generated by thousands of privately owned banks competing for market share in a large, heterogeneous, and rapidly integrating

[20] Between 1921 and 1929, there were 5,712 bank failures, an average of nearly two banks per day. Author's calculation based on FDIC Historical Statistics (FDIC, 2002).

economy. It was just too tempting for banks (and states) to manipulate the money supply to accommodate local preferences or their own competitive objectives, ignoring the systemic effect of their actions. While the states loathed relinquishing their regulatory prerogatives to the Federal government, the coordination problems that emerged from economic integration and industrialization so imperiled the stability of local political economies that states found it in their interests to make some regulatory concessions.[21] The decade of the 1970's marks a new era of threats to safety and soundness in the banking system, new coordination problems, a renewed interest in market coordination, and significant institutional change.

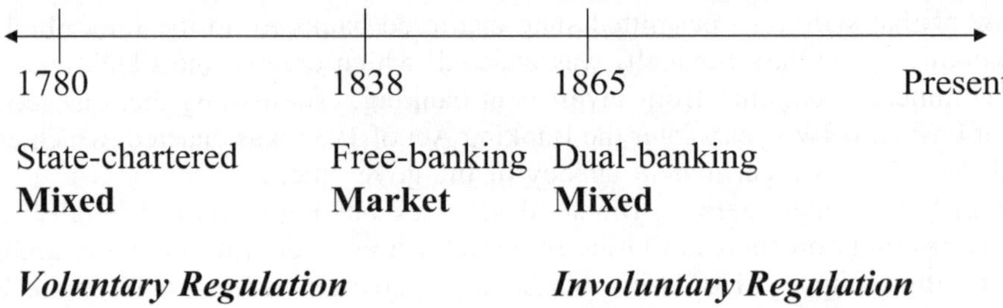

Figure 5.2. The Evolution of Banking Institutions.

Institutional Change

Responding to the economic changes in the financial services environment that are described in Chapter Four required new business and regulatory strategies: implementing these strategies required institutional change in both the private and the public sectors. And so beginning in the 1970s, commercial banks and their regulators embarked upon a long period of institutional change that culminated in formally repealing many of the restraints on powers that were enacted in response to the economic crises of the 1920s and 1930s. Banks, trade associations, regulators, and legislators worked tirelessly to reform banking regulations and laws. These efforts and processes are well described in the banking literature. However, *de jure* change is not the only way that institutional change occurs: change can also occur *de facto* by reorganizing the firm to compete in new ways that are not prohibited by law, ceasing to monitor and enforce against an existing rule, or interpreting a rule in a new or more liberal manner. Substantively and procedurally, both types of institutional change are possible in the U.S. banking system yet neither the theoretical nor empirical literature addresses *de facto* change processes. As the following analysis will demonstrate, it turns out that there is considerable latitude

[21] Note that this is a pattern of institutional compromise in the United States that is impervious to political activity. Originating in colonial times and repeated in many different areas of activity over the past 250 years, it is more a function of the structure of governance than of tradition. Chapters Four and Six elaborate on this phenomenon.

for *de facto* change in the U.S. commercial banking system. Moreover, this is where the real action is in banking reform in the late 20th century.

Institutional Change in the Private Sector

Changes in the financial services environment put banks at a disadvantage because banking laws prohibited them from diversifying geographically and limited the range of financial products and services they could offer. However, there are several ways that firms can potentially cope with regulatory constraints: 1) they can change the identity of the firm, 2) they can implement process innovations, or 3) they can implement product or service innovations. While commercial banks may have attempted to use all three strategies to transcend regulatory constraints, there is limited evidence that they successfully implemented significant product or service innovations over the period under investigation in this study, and so the following section focuses on identity and process innovations.[22]

Identity

Recall from Chapter Four that firms that were legally defined as banks faced competition from firms that were not legally defined as banks. Firms that had alternative identities, such as finance companies, mutual funds, or non-bank banks, had broader powers and faced fewer restrictions on their activities. The competitive challenge for banks was to expand their powers without leaving the banking business: they initially met this challenge by forming Bank Holding Companies (BHCs) and more recently, by forming Financial Holding Companies (FHCs).

A BHC is a legal entity that owns one or more banks but is not defined as a bank under banking law. As long as states permitted the formation of BHCs (most did), this organizational form could be used to expand the size and scope of financial services activities, avoid certain restrictions on powers imposed by state and federal banking authorities, reduce the costs of regulatory compliance, and reduce tax payments. This was accomplished by reorganizing provision and production activities into separate subsidiaries, taking care to avoid endowing the subsidiary with the characteristics of a "branch" as defined under the McFadden Act. In this way deposit-taking and commercial lending activities could be owned in common and bank and non-bank financial services could be consolidated in one financial entity.[23] BHCs that owned more than one bank in a state could sidestep unit-

---

[22] Product innovation is a challenge that banks have yet to whole-heartedly address. For a critique of banks innovative capacity, see Drucker, 1999.

[23] Under U.S. corporate laws, common ownership does not imply common governance or centralization of decision-making authority: laws permit corporate entities to organize and govern using a range of structures from highly centralized, hierarchical structures to polycentric structures in which subsidiary units compete for investment capital and other resources. In a study that is relevant to the period that is investigated here, Rose (1978) finds that the amount of control exercised over bank subsidiaries varies sharply across BHCs from limited control to very tight control that

banking restrictions and effectively engage in branch banking.[24] In addition to product and geographic diversification, the firms owned by a BHC could realize other competitive advantages compared to independent or unit banks, such as economies of scale, raising funds free of Regulation Q restrictions on interest rate payments, and avoiding Regulation D reserve requirements. The formation of BHCs also provided banks with the financial strength they needed to expand their geographic and market scope by making mergers and acquisitions and investing in new information processing technologies.

BHC statistics over the period 1960–2000 demonstrate the extent to which the industry embarked upon identity change. In 1960, 217 BHCs controlled 11.1% of commercial banking assets. After 1965, both the number of BHCs and the percentage of assets controlled by BHCs increased dramatically: in 1970, 1,321 BHCs controlled 16.2% of assets and by 1990, 6,425 BHCs controlled 94% of assets.[25] The growth of BHCs was most pronounced in two periods: 1960–1967 and 1977–1989. The first period coincides with the formation of BHCs by non-bank entities and the emergence of new competition in financial services. The second period coincides with a sharp increase in the price of money and the period in which all but eight states passed legislation that enabled some form of interstate banking through BHCs.

With the passage of the Graham Leach Bliley Act of 1999, which concludes the period of institutional change that is investigated in this study, BHCs and foreign banking organizations that qualify as FHCs may engage in a broad range of activities that are financial in nature or incidental to financial activities. As of December 31, 2000, 463 domestic BHCs and 21 foreign banking organizations had received FHC status. Of the 463 domestic FHCs, 32 had consolidated assets of $15 billion or more; 59 had assets of $1–15 billion; 34 had assets of $500 million – $1 billion; 338 had assets of less than $500 million.[26]

Mergers and acquisitions (M&A), which are analyzed in more detail in Chapter Four, are another way to change identity: the growth of M&A activity is closely

---

approximates that of a branch system. He argues that in general, parent companies and their banking subsidiaries have a shared management philosophy and broadly consistent operating policies. Organization structure is decentralized and the parent extends considerable operating autonomy to the subsidiary, contingent upon meeting profit expectations. Subsidiaries have the most autonomy in setting prices, evaluating loan applications, and managing human resources. They have the least autonomy in securities and federal funds management, correspondent banking relations outside the BHC, capital management, and *de novo* expansion.

[24] For studies of the use of the BHC form see Lawrence (1967), Association of Registered Bank Holding Companies (1973), Boczar (1975), Board of Governors of the Federal Reserve (1978), Savage (1978) and Rhoades and Rutz (1979). Forming as an Edge Act Corporation, which must engage in international or foreign banking but can establish branches across state lines, was another organizational option. For a comprehensive discussion of the legal issues involved in structuring activities to expand geographic scope, see Ginsburg (1981). More detailed discussion of the use of BHCs appears in the section on institutional change in the public sector.

[25] Author's compilation based on Savage, 1978, and Annual Reports of the Board of Governors of the Federal Reserve.

[26] Author's estimate based on Federal Reserve statistics.

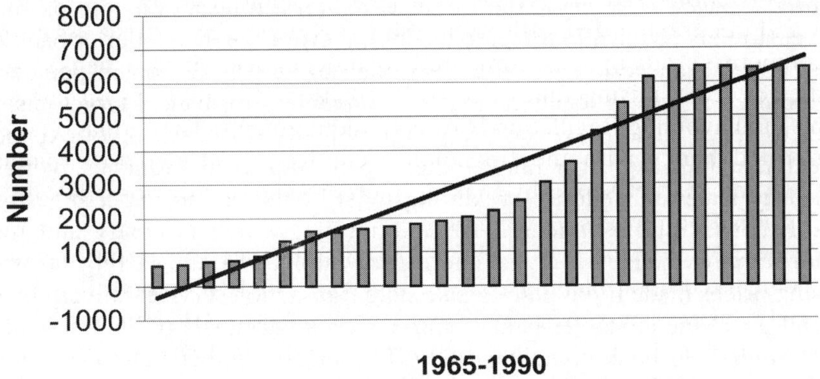

Figure 5.3. Bank Holding Companies.

Source: Author's estimate based on Federal Reserve statistics and Boczar (1975).

related to formation of BHCs and liberalization of geographic restrictions on banking activities. Over the period 1980–1998, there were 8,000 commercial bank mergers and holding company acquisitions involving more than $2.4 trillion in assets (Rhoades, 2000). In general, when a firm merges with or acquires another firm, the combination brings previously independent entities under common ownership and expands the financial base of the firm. Mergers and acquisitions are a quick way to increase the scale and scope of activities. In addition, there are a number of other reasons why bank managers might engage in M&A activity: mergers and acquisitions that increase market power increase the value of the bank and depending upon industry conditions, may allow banks to set prices, lower costs, or provide new products and services; when there is excess capacity in an industry, mergers are a means to avert cutthroat rivalry; they can be a defensive reaction to competitors' M&A activity; they are also a means by which managers can enhance their reputations or protect their personal interests.[27]

Process Innovation

The other way that banks overcame regulatory restrictions to compete effectively was by finding new ways to produce and provide services that improved returns. The two principle types of process innovations that commercial banks successfully implemented in the late 20th century are automated service delivery, which reduces the costs of transaction processing and improves customer service, and financial engineering, which frees capital for investment in alternative lines of business.

[27] In a year-by-year study of consolidation in the financial services industry over the period 1985–1997, Berger, Demsetz, and Strahan (1998) find evidence that consolidation has had both positive and negative efficiency effects.

Automated Service Delivery. Traditionally, banking transactions are executed in person: customers physically travel to a banking office where a teller or bank officer processes their transaction requests. Service delivery based on in-person transacting requires offices in locations that are convenient for banks' target customers. In order to serve customers who are geographically dispersed or to expand geographically, a banking firm must either open additional branches, which was restricted by state and federal law during most of the period under investigation, or establish subsidiaries under a BHC umbrella, which is costly and requires regulatory approval. However, technological innovation and falling information processing prices made it possible to automate transaction service delivery by developing and installing customer-bank communication terminals (CBCTs), which link remote terminals to bank computers. CBCTs include terminals and CRTs installed in corporate customers' offices, Automated Teller Machines (ATMs), and Point of Sale (POS) devices.

Installation of CBCTs at corporate customers' offices is a relatively small, specialized market related to delivering corporate cash management services. Similarly, the installation of POS devices, which are typically installed in retail establishments, has a relatively limited impact on transaction processing activities. However, installation of ATMs, which are unattended CBCTs that permit retail bank customers to make deposits, withdraw cash, transfer funds between accounts, and make loan payments, provide banks with a significant competitive advantage in transaction processing on a very large scale. By developing regional and national ATM networks, which were generally permissible over a wider geographic area than branches, banks legally expanded the scale and geographic scope of business activities at relatively low cost.[28]

The use of ATM networks to overcome regulatory restrictions on branching is demonstrated by the growth of ATM networks, which were first developed in the 1970s. Over the period 1978–1995, the number of ATMs increased from 9,750 to nearly 123,000. The most intense periods of growth in the use of ATMs occurred between 1982 and 1989, and from 1993 to 1995. The first period precedes substantial liberalization in state branching laws. The second period coincides with federal liberalization of interstate banking laws.

Even as restrictions on powers were diminishing in the 1990s, commercial banks continued to innovate to reduce costs and improve services in transaction processing by offering debit cards, electronic banking, and electronic payment services. The

---

[28] There are two ways that banks have organized ATM-based service delivery. They have owned and managed exclusive (unshared) networks of ATMs, and they have participated in networks with other banks. Shared ATM networks can be owned and managed by one bank, a joint venture among banks, a non-bank subsidiary of a BHC, or a computer communications network company unaffiliated with any bank or BHC. Each of these arrangements has different implications for determining whether an ATM network is subject to branching restrictions under state and federal laws. In order to avoid running afoul of interstate and intrastate branching restrictions, ATM deposit-taking was generally restricted to permit deposits only at ATMs in the state of the customer's own bank. See Ginsburg (1981) for an analysis of the legal status of CBCTs and strategic use of these devices to expand the geographic scope of banking activities.

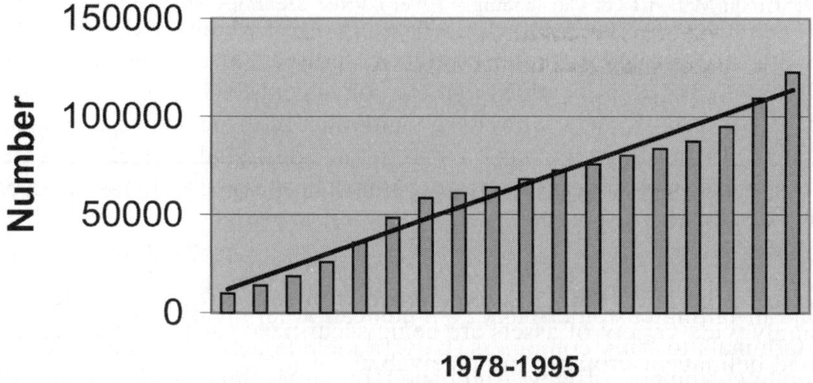

Figure 5.4. ATM Installations.

Source: Author's estimate based on Berger, et al. (1995) and Kroszner and Strahan (1998).

total volume of debit card transactions increased from $12 million in 1990 to $322 million in 1999. Similarly, the volume of electronic payments increased from $20 billion or 0.7% of all consumer payments in 1990 to $723 billion or 10.7% of all payments in 1999.[29]

Financial Engineering. Financial engineering is another way in which banks sought to improve their competitive position in financial services and cope with regulatory restrictions. Securitization, which is the process of pooling assets with similar cash flow characteristics and repackaging them in a pool in a way that permits the originator to sell security interests, is the first of two significant innovations in bank finance. Beginning in 1970, banks began to securitize their loan portfolios in order to better allocate the risk associated with credit initiation.[30] Loan securitization dramatically altered the way that banks do business. By selling loans that they previously held to maturity and thus removing risky assets from their balance sheet and freeing up capital to support additional lending, banks have been able to replace the prime lending business they have lost due to disintermediation with sub-prime lending. While home mortgages were the first loans to be securitized, non-mortgage assets, such as auto loans and credit card receivables, were

---

[29] Data source is U.S. Census Bureau, Statistical Abstract of the United States: 2001, No. 1188 and 1189. For overviews of electronic finance activities, see Horovitz and White (1998), Allen, McAndrews, and Strahan (2001) and Sato, Hawkins, and Berentsen (2001).

[30] Securitization produces asset-backed securities that provide the investor with a right to collect the financial value of the underlying assets. Typically, principal and interest cash flows are paid to investors in the pool, who are usually large institutions. The investors assume the prepayment risk of the underlying assets. Most deals are very large, include some type of credit enhancement, and offer yields that exceed those on comparable corporate bonds. Hence, asset backed securities tend to be quite liquid. For a review of developments in banks' use of securitization, see Feldman (1995).

Table 5.1. Credit Market Debt Outstanding – Asset Backed Securities Issuers

Item	1980	1985	1990	1995	2000
Credit Market	4,733	8,629	13,755	18,445	27,514
ABS Issuers	–	37	271	713	1,838

Source: U.S. Census Bureau, Statistical Abstract of the United States 2001, Section 25, No. 1165 (Billions of U.S. Dollars).

securitized in the mid-1980s. As experience with securitization has deepened, an increasingly wide variety of assets are being securitized such as boat loans, student loans, and delinquent property tax receivables.

The second significant innovation that has affected bank finance is the use of derivatives to structure financial risk. Derivatives are contracts that give one party a claim on an underlying asset (or the cash value of the asset) at some point in the future, and bind another party to meet a corresponding liability.[31] While derivatives were actively traded in the 17th century in both Amsterdam and New Amsterdam (New York City) to facilitate trading when time lags were involved in a transaction, modern use of financial derivatives in the U.S. can be traced to the GNMA futures contract, which began trading in the 1970s (Light, 1995).[32] The GNMA was developed by financial institutions to contend with the increased volatility of interest rates, which made holding mortgages riskier. Today, banks routinely use derivative contracts to reduce risk, change the nature of financial exposure, and to reduce transaction costs connected with managing foreign exchange and interest rate risks. Edwards and Mishkin (1995) argue that in addition to using derivatives for risk management, banks use them to offset the shortfall in profits coming from their traditional business. Von Hagen and Fender (1998), who analyze growth in the use of derivatives, estimate that banks have become the dominant group of dealers on derivatives markets.

Institutional Change in the Public Sector

The polycentric structure of commercial banking regulation dictates three general approaches to reforming public banking rules, each of which are subject to legal challenge: (1) Congress can amend an existing law or make new law that supercedes state laws, (2) the states can make permissive law, and (3) regulators can use their administrative authority to reinterpret an existing law, either relaxing enforcement of the rule or tightening enforcement. This means that institutional change in the

[31] A derivatives contract may rest on an amount of currency, a security, a physical commodity, a stream of payments or a market index. It may bind the parties equally or offer one party the option to exercise or not. It may require a swap of assets or liabilities, or it may combine several elements. For an overview of the use of derivatives, see Minehan and Simons (1995).

[32] For a history of financial activities in New Amsterdam and the origins of New York City as an international financial center, see Gordon, 1999.

public sector can occur in approximately 108 separate but strategically interdependent fora: the U.S. Congress, fifty state legislatures, the Executive branch of federal government (through the Office of the Comptroller of the Currency, which is in the Department of the Treasury, and the Federal Trade Commission, which is in the Department of Justice), two federal regulators (the Federal Reserve and the FDIC), fifty state regulators, and three court systems (state, federal, and Supreme).

While banking specialists like to complain that the complex structure of U.S. banking regulation makes it very difficult to change banking regulation, the evidence to support this assertion is contradictory. As the first section of this chapter argues, it was quite difficult to regulate money and banking in the first instance: the nation was nearly a century old before it was able to begin to implement stable controls. However, since that time, banking regulation shows considerable flexibility, particularly in response to significant structural change in the U.S. economy: in the twentieth century, there are two periods of intense institutional change in U.S. banking: 1913–1935 and 1966–1999. Over the period investigated in this study, Congress enacted 16 federal laws pertaining to banking and the states enacted at least 50 laws.[33]

A quick review of findings thus far makes it possible to simplify the analysis. Beginning in the 1970s, competitive rivalry in financial services increased markedly. In responding to competition, the key collective action problem for banks was to remove regulatory restraints on powers that restricted them from expanding geographically or diversifying their product and service offerings. They coped with these restrictions by reorganizing as Bank Holding Companies, engaging in an unprecedented amount of merger and acquisition activity, automating transaction processing, and re-engineering the structure of their assets. Hence, the institutional changes in

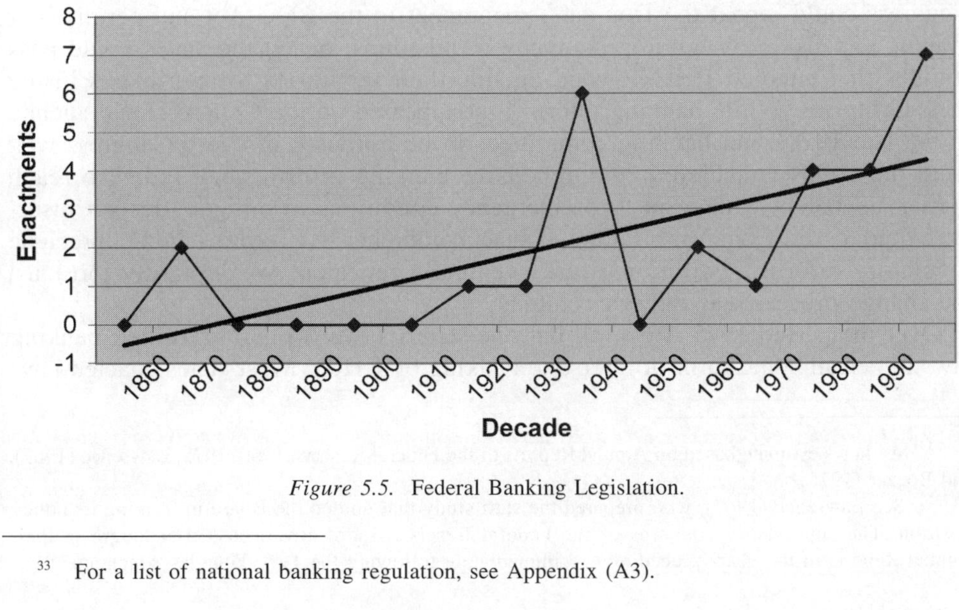

Figure 5.5. Federal Banking Legislation.

[33] For a list of national banking regulation, see Appendix (A3).

the public sector that are most relevant to solving collective action problems associated with responding to competition in the financial services industry are changes that affect branching and diversification, including statutory change at state and federal levels and supervisory actions by regulators who had authority over the formation of BHCs, the approval of bank mergers and acquisitions, transaction processing innovations, and balance sheet composition.

Statutory Change

Statutory change in the late 20th century begins with the enactment of the Douglas Amendments to the Bank Holding Company Act in 1970. Exploiting the loophole in the BHC Act that excluded One Bank Holding Companies (OBHCs) from regulation, banks formed OBHCs in the 1960s in order to expand into real estate, brokerage, and securities underwriting activities, and non-bank enterprises formed them to expand into banking: the number of OBHCs increased from approximately 170 in 1960 to 1,200 by 1970.[34] Observing this trend and its implications for evading restraints on powers in banking, the Federal Reserve asked Congress to amend the Bank Holding Company Act to include OBHCs.[35] This was swiftly accomplished and in 1970, The Douglas Amendment was enacted, which effectively eliminated the distinction between OBHCs and MBHCs, expanded the Federal Reserve's regulatory discretion, and explicitly granted states the power to establish laws regarding interstate bank holding company expansion. Under the terms of this amendment, a BHC could branch across state lines if specifically authorized by state statute. At the time, no state had such a statute.

After the Douglas Amendment was enacted in 1970, there were three ways to reform banking regulation in the U.S.: (1) Congress could repeal the McFadden Act to allow *de novo* branching expansion, and the Glass Steagall Act to remove the separation between banking and other types of financial services activities, (2) Congress could repeal the Douglas Amendment to the BHC Act and permit geographic expansion by holding company acquisitions, or (3) the states could pass statutes that enabled BHCs owned outside their territories to own banks inside their territories. While banking reform first appeared on the Congressional agenda in the late 1970s and banking committees in both houses in every Congress well in to the 1990s considered comprehensive banking reform, they failed to reach consensus except with respect to emergency conditions to mitigate deposit insurance fund losses. Congress's failure to enact comprehensive reforms did not preclude regulatory reform: restrictions were eventually repealed. While hardly tortuous, the change process was rather circuitous.

Over the period 1975–1994, all but one state (Hawaii) liberalized their banking laws to permit some form of interstate banking by BHCs. Most states enacted laws

---

[34] Author's estimate based on Annual Reports of the Federal Reserve 1960–1975, Lawrence (1967), and Boczar (1975).

[35] See Lawrence (1967), who prepared the staff study that guided the Board in forming its policy position. The supervisory concerns of the Federal Reserve Board are discussed at length in their Annual Reports in the years preceding and immediately following the 1970 Douglas Amendment.

in the three-year period 1984–1987, when the number of states with permissive statutes increased from two to thirty three. By the time federal regulation passed in 1994, interstate banking already existed in the U.S. largely as a function of reforms made by the states and liberal decisions taken by federal bank regulators.[36] A Supreme Court ruling in 1985 on the constitutionality of regional interstate banking compacts simultaneously took the pressure off of Congress to act on interstate banking reform and served to stimulate state legislative action.[37]

The states approached interstate banking reform incrementally. Initially, they formed regional interstate banking compacts and passed regional reciprocal statutes. These statutes permitted bank acquisitions by BHCs located in one of a designated group of regional state partners, providing that the BHC's home state allowed reciprocal privileges. However, by 1987, most states had further liberalized their interstate banking laws to permit nationwide privileges. For example, in 1985, 14 states had interstate banking statutes. Of these 14 states, 9 permitted interstate banking on a regional reciprocal basis, three permitted it on a nationwide basis, and two permitted it on a regional reciprocal basis with a trigger to nationwide.[38] By the end of 1987, 33 states permitted interstate banking: 15 on a regional reciprocal basis, 9 on a nationwide basis, and 9 on a regional basis with a trigger to nationwide. By the end of 1988, only eight states had no interstate banking statute and the majority of statutes permitted interstate banking either on a nationwide basis or on a regional reciprocal basis with a trigger to nationwide. When Congress passed the Interstate Bank Branching and Efficiency Act of 1994 (Reigle Neal Act), interstate banking had already been implemented: rather than enact interstate banking, federal legislation simply served to harmonize disparities in state statues.[39]

The states could implement interstate banking reform, however they could not unilaterally remove restrictions on powers, which were largely regulated by federal banking laws. While Congress did not repeal restrictions on powers until 1999, they did attempt to level the competitive playing field as a means to address the banking crises in the both the Savings and Loan and commercial banking industries. In addition to restrictions on diversification, banks could not raise interest rates

---

[36] Berger, Kashyap, and Scalise (1995) estimate that the average potential geographic reach of an MBHC rose from 6.5% in 1979 to 69.4% in 1994, implying that by 1994 the typical MBHC already had the legal right to operate in states accounting for 69.4% of the nation's banking assets.

[37] In *Northeast Bancorp, Inc. v. Board of Governors of the Federal Reserve System* (No. 84-363 June 10, 1985), the Supreme Court ruled that regional interstate banking compacts are permitted under the U.S. Constitution.

[38] A trigger is a specified time limit or a sequence of events for national entry rights to become effective.

[39] There were many differences in the provisions of state interstate banking statutes. Common provisions pertained to the type or mode of entry, the design of a region, anti-leapfrogging (in regional agreements, prevents banking firms whose principal place of business is outside the region from entering a state by acquiring a bank in another state that is part of the region), reciprocity, triggers, type of institutions, and opt-outs (allows home state banks to declare themselves immune from interstate banking for a specified period). The IBBEA harmonized the essential features of these laws while giving states the right to either opt-in earlier than the statute provided for or opt-out entirely by a specified time. Most states elected to opt-in early.

Table 5.2. Changes in Interstate Banking Regulation

Year Effective	Nationwide or Regional Reciprocal with Trigger	Regional Reciprocal (No Trigger)	No Action
1978	1	0	50
1979	1	0	50
1980	1	0	50
1981	1	0	50
1982	3	0	48
1983	3	2	46
1984	3	0	48
1985	5	9	37
1986	11	12	28
1987	18	15	18
1988	27	16	8
1989	27	17	7
1990	29	17	5

Source: Author's estimate based on Conference of State Bank Supervisors (August, 1988).

on transaction accounts above a specified ceiling until 1980, and until 1982 they could not offer money market accounts or interest on commercial checking accounts. Congress enacted the Depository Institutions Deregulation and Monetary Control Act of 1980, which mandated that interest rate ceilings (regulation Q) be phased out by March 1986. However, this change was not sufficient to staunch the loss of depositors so in 1982, Congress passed the Depository Institutions Act (Garn-St. Germain), which authorized banks to offer money market deposit accounts exempt from regulation Q ceilings (Berger, Kashyap, and Scalise, 1995).

While deposit-rate deregulation was intended to make it easier for banks to compete for deposits with other financial services providers, it was a mixed blessing. When deposit rates were deregulated, banks were indeed able to better compete against other financial service providers who were providing superior substitutes, however, it also increased their cost of funds, which reduced the competitive advantage of both taking deposits and making loans. In other words, it reduced the advantage of being a bank. Interest rate volatility exacerbated the problem by making it difficult to keep loan rates and deposit rates in sync so that banks could maintain adequate liquidity. Berger, Kashyap, and Scalise (1995) report that as of 1979, total bank interest expenses were 5.48 percentage points below the average one-year Treasury rate for the same year. By 1986, when deposit interest rates were totally deregulated, the interest expense ratio was only 1.32 percent below the Treasury rate of 6.45%. This is an increase in interest costs of 4.16% of assets, which reflects a significant loss of competitive advantage.

In related developments, Congress began to deregulate other aspects of pricing and powers in the banking industry. The Depository Institutions Deregulation and Monetary Control Act of 1980 gradually phased out the legal ceiling rates on deposits sold to the public and permitted federally insured banks to offer interest-bearing checking accounts to all customers. The Garn-St. Germain Depository Institutions Act of 1982 permitted banks and non-bank thrifts to offer money market deposit accounts in order to compete with the share accounts offered by money market mutual funds. Both of these acts were efforts to level the playing field between banks and other financial service providers. State regulators pursued a deregulatory stance as well. While legislators struggled to find consensus for banking reform, more rapid strides were made in removing restrictions on powers by means of regulatory relaxation than statutory change.

Regulatory Relaxation

The stance that regulators take with respect to interpretation and enforcement of existing law is an important signal to those who have an interest in the affairs of a regulated industry. Regulatory stance indicates the types of institutional change that are permissible on a formal and discretionary basis. As long as the economic environment of an industry is stable, there is little reason to expect a change in regulatory stance. However, economic changes that present new opportunities or threats provide an opportunity for firms to attempt to expand their scope of activities by arguing that prior positions and rulings no longer apply or are no longer effective in achieving regulatory goals. Regulators must then reassess their position. In the U.S. system, aggressive firms can achieve competitive advantage by successfully challenging regulatory constraints: aggrieved competitors and other interest groups are left to seek redress in the courts and political arenas.

There are four interrelated ways that regulators used their discretion to permit banks to diversify. First, they approved an unprecedented number of BHC applications and liberally construed permissible activities. Second, they not only approved an equally unprecedented number of mergers and acquisitions, they aggressively encouraged healthy banks to acquire the assets of their weaker competitors. Third, they liberally granted new banking charters as a means to increase competition in the industry, and finally, they used their discretion to permit banks to engage in activities that were beyond the traditional purview of banking.

As the BHC statistics demonstrate, banks aggressively applied to reorganize as BHCs and the Federal Reserve just as aggressively approved their applications. Before 1970, one-bank holding companies could avoid regulatory supervision all together. While the 1970 Amendments to the BHC Act eliminated this opportunity, it gave the Federal Reserve discretion to determine whether an activity proposed by a BHC was "closely related to banking," and "reasonably expected to produce benefits to the public . . . that outweigh possible adverse effects." Initially, the Federal Reserve hewed rather closely to the letter of the Bank Holding Company Act and the perceived intent of Congress to dampen diversification using the BHC form.[40] It permitted BHCs to expand into consumer lending activities but not into deposit-taking activities. However, as competition in the financial services industry

---

[40] For a more extensive discussion of the Federal Reserve's supervision of BHCs, see Golembe and Associates (1979).

intensified and bank failures increased, the Federal Reserve expanded the list of permissible banking activities for well-capitalized BHCs.

In the U.S., banks can only merge with or be acquired by other banks, and M&A activity is heavily regulated by multiple laws and multiple regulatory authorities.[41] Three laws primarily govern mergers and acquisitions in the banking industry: The Banking Holding Company Act of 1956 and 1970 amendments, the Bank Merger Act of 1960, and the Change in Bank Control Act of 1978.[42]

The Bank Merger Act requires that all proposed bank mergers between insured banks receive prior approval from the agency under whose jurisdiction the surviving bank will fall. It also sets forth the factors to be considered in evaluating merger applications. The Change in Bank Control Act gives the Federal Reserve responsibility for changes in the control of BHCs and state member banks, the Federal Deposit Insurance Corporation (FDIC) for changes in insured state nonmember banks, and the Office of the Comptroller of the Currency (OCC) responsibility for changes in the control of national banks. In considering changes in bank control, the law prohibits regulators from approving a merger or acquisition that substantially lessens competition unless the benefits of doing so out weigh the social costs. In addition, they must review factors such as the financial condition, competence, experience, and integrity of the acquiring person or group and the adequacy of the information provided by the party proposing the change. Finally, the provisions of the Community Reinvestment Act of 1977 require the Federal Reserve to consider a bank's record in community investment in approving a merger or acquisition.

From the late 1970s through the mid-1980s, a number of decisions by the Federal Reserve, the courts, and the Justice Department, moved policy toward permitting mergers and acquisitions that would have been denied in previous years. For example, the Justice Department and the Federal Reserve began allowing bank mergers in highly concentrated markets on the assumption that banks faced substantial competition from non-bank financial intermediaries. Between 1979 and 1994, the percentage of deposits held by subsidiaries of out of state BHCs in the typical state expanded from 2% to 27.9%.[43]

The financial crisis in the banking industry in the 1980s stimulated further regulatory relaxation, which was intended to rescue failing banks and to create incentives for large banks to reduce risk by increasing capital ratios. Over the period 1984–1991, the FDIC provided assistance to well-capitalized BHCs to allow them to purchase more than 1,000 insolvent banks. Evanoff and Fortier (1986) argue

---

[41] In addition to anti-competitive concerns and assuring compliance with goals specified under the Community Reinvestment Act, the role of government in regulating M&A activity in the banking industry is related to limiting government (taxpayer) liability and preventing the moral hazard that arises as a function of providing deposit insurance.

[42] Congress created an exception to these rules as a means to manage the systemic threat of burgeoning bank failures. The Depository Institutions Act of 1982 (Garn-St. Germain) permits the FDIC and the Federal Savings and Loan Insurance Corporation (FSLIC) to approve interstate and inter-industry mergers and acquisitions to aid troubled thrifts and banks.

[43] For a more extensive discussion of these developments, see Berger, Kashyap, and Scalise (1995).

that the Act was the mechanism for four of the nation's largest BHCs to gain an interstate presence that could not have been achieved under the Douglas Amendment.

In the 1980s, both the OCC and the states sharply increased chartering as a means to stimulate banking reform. Texas – where intrastate branching was restricted – accounted for particularly large shares of new state and national bank charters. In 1980, the OCC revised its requirements for approving new charters, specifically seeking to foster increased competition by allowing new entrants into banking markets. However, a disproportionate number of new banks became troubled, causing the FDIC to raise a red flag about liberal chartering: the number of new commercial bank charters reached a peak in 1984 and then gradually declined until 1994 (FDIC, 1997).

In addition to using their discretion to encourage bank reform through liberal chartering, the OCC and the states took a liberal stance toward diversification of banking activities. The OCC issued several rulings that took a narrow interpretation of "branch" under McFadden and permitted banks to develop loan production offices, ATM networks, and armored car services. Although the courts subsequently disapproved each of these rulings, these activities were often permitted at the state level (Ginsburg, 1981).

Summary

The complexity of U.S. governance processes is a favorite scapegoat for performance problems in the U.S. banking industry. Economists and bankers alike contend that "politics" inhibit growth and development in the banking sector. They argue that it is difficult to summon the political will to change existing regulations or agree to new regulations when economic conditions change, and so we should regulate banking quite differently. However, politics emerge from governance structure and so what my colleagues are really complaining about is the constitutional structure of U.S. banking regulation, which, like that of the nation as a whole, is polycentric. Yet the evidence that this governance structure has failed to successfully facilitate adaptive economic and institutional change is rather sparse. Instead, this survey of institutional change over the period 1960–2000 suggests that there is considerable latitude in the U.S. banking system for change but it occurs in both the private and public sectors and the process is evolutionary rather than revolutionary.

As forces in the economic environment produced new competition, extensive structural change, and eroded market share in traditional service segments, the banking industry not only adapted, it prospered: revenues as a share of all private industry GDP increased from about 2% in 1960 to over 4% in 2000. Rather than being stymied by restrictions, bank managers implemented extensive innovations that affected the structure of the banking business, the nature of the business, and the way in which business is conducted. Regulators and legislators reformed deeply entrenched rules, some of which had been in place for over 250 years. And despite bank failures in numbers not seen since the Great Depression, no depositor lost

Table 5.3. Gross Domestic Product of Depository Institutions 1960–2000

GDP (Millions of $)	1960	%	2000	%
All Private Industries	442,116	100	8,656,499	100
Depository Institutions	8,162	1.85	366,469	4.23

Source: U.S. Bureau of Economic Analysis GDP Statistics.

any federally insured funds, there was no significant disruption of the financial intermediation process, and financial market stability was maintained.

The process of commercial banking reform did not occur quickly nor was it controlled by any single participant: everyone participated including consumers and potential competitors.[44] However, firms rather than governments led the institutional change process. Executive branch staff, regulators, and legislators assumed leadership roles in facilitating discussion and debate however, institutional change was initiated and implemented by firms responding to changes in their economic environment. Many (but not all) banking firms took action before the direction of regulatory change was certain, despite the potential for failure or a disabling challenge. The changes they made reconfigured the types of firms operating in the financial services industry and reflect changes in beliefs about competing effectively in the banking business.

Institutional change in the public sector coincided with and responded to structural change in financial services markets, pre-emptive change in the private sector, and the threat of systemic crisis. By the time regulators and legislators formally liberalized restrictions on banking activities, there was clear evidence of competition from non-bank financial enterprises, a shift in demand away from traditional banking relationships, and financial stress in the industry. However, while changes in competition in financial services convinced many state bank regulators that regulatory reform was necessary and stimulated change at local levels, institutional change at the national level appears to have responded more to systemic threats than to competition *per se*. Now that we have an overview of the economic and institutional changes that actually occurred over the period 1960–2000, we can return to theoretical questions about the causes and processes of change.

---

[44] In addition to extensive Congressional hearings (U.S. Government), there were many studies conducted by governments, regulators, academics, and other policy researchers. See for example Baer and Gregorash, eds. (1986), Haraf and Kushmeider, eds. (1988), U.S. Department of the Treasury (1993), and Klausner and White (1993).

CHAPTER SIX

Explaining Commercial Banking Reform

Armed with some facts about the actual nature of economic and institutional change in the U.S. commercial banking industry, we can now return to the challenge of explaining what happened and why it happened as it did. Recall that Chapter Three set up several sets of questions and theoretical assumptions about change. The first set of questions has to do with understanding the stimulus for change in a regulated industry – what motivates the process, whether it is a response to a failure or an opportunity, and if it is in response to a failure, the source of the failure. The second set of questions has to do with the process of change, including types of economic and institutional change, participants, motivations, the role of competition, and coordination mechanisms. Integrating theory and empirical evidence on change, it was proposed that economic and institutional change is an adaptive process in response to an economic or institutional shock that involves simultaneous change in multiple sectors of activity. Successful adaptation is conditioned upon participants having the ability to conceptualize and implement change, flexible "rules of the game," and adequate resources to implement changes in governance and economizing. This idea is expressed by four assumptions about economic and institutional change in regulated industries in the U.S.:

A1: Change is stimulated by a shock or set of shocks in the economic or institutional environment that alters beliefs about opportunities or threats to maintaining the status quo in the industry. Providing that certain conditions associated with successful implementation are met, shocks will stimulate change in the private and public sectors.

A2: Beliefs about opportunities, which are reflected in decision making and collective action in the private and public sectors, change.

A3: Governance changes

A4: Economizing changes

Chapters Four and Five provide a great deal of evidence that suggests that in U.S. commercial banking, economic and institutional change is indeed an adaptive process that involves simultaneous activity in many sectors. Moreover, some firms succeed while others fail, indicating that there is set of conditions upon which successful adaptation depends. Finally, change is incremental and takes place over time.

Chapter Four provides evidence that commercial banking reform was motivated by shocks in both the economic and institutional environments that created new opportunities in financial services markets. Hence activities in both environments are potentially important sources of change. Interestingly, neither markets, nor governments, nor institutions failed in *toto*: each type of coordinating mechanism played and continues to play an important role in regulating commercial banking activities in the U.S. and in motivating and managing change. This is not to say that these mechanisms functioned perfectly: there were rigidities in all three areas: banking reform provides a number of lessons about the strengths and weaknesses of these mechanisms.[1] However the relevant point in this study is that adaptive change in financial services involves all three types of coordination mechanisms rather than just one. Hence the oft-expressed choice between markets, governments, or institutions is a false choice in the U.S. political economy and a misleading simplification in research.

Changes in beliefs about the competitive environment of banking were directly expressed in public debates, the business press, and various reports, and indirectly expressed in the decision making and collective behavior of regulators, policy makers, and bank managers, which can be inferred from events and the evolution of the industry over time. Firms and regulators were aware of the need to consider reform, debated reform, and implemented reforms that reflect changes in beliefs about the best way to effectively compete in the industry. Changes in the structure, conduct, and performance of the banking industry demonstrate the impact of the evolution of beliefs as well as the ability of a significant number of firms in the industry to meet the conditions hypothesized to be associated with successful adaptation: sufficient ability, institutional flexibility, and adequate resources.

Chapter Five provides evidence of changes in governance in the public and private sectors that coincide with changes in the economic and institutional environment of commercial banking. Firms in the private sector took the lead in adaptive change. They coped with rigidities in bank regulation with both firm-level and collective action. At the firm level, bank managers reorganized as bank holding companies and implemented process innovations that changed the way they were regulated and allowed them to compete more effectively. At the same time, they worked with other firms in their industry to craft solutions to common problems, lobby for change, and reform existing laws. As competition and regulatory constraints took their toll, regulators and legislators responded by easing restrictions on diversification. Regulators used their discretion to liberally interpret existing law and relax restrictions on the activities of well-capitalized bank holding companies, and state legislators removed restrictions at local levels. Once consensus on the direction of

---

[1] For a detailed analysis of lessons that can be drawn from the bank crises of the 1980s and early 1990s, see FDIC (1997).

change had been reached, federal legislators enacted laws that harmonized changes that had been made at local levels.

Evidence about the financial performance of the banking industry presented in Chapter Four suggests that changes in economizing are also associated with changes in the institutional and economic environment of commercial banking. However, the nature of these changes may not be consistent with standard theory or transaction cost economics: aggregate data on industry performance suggests that despite increased competition and institutional change, banks may not have improved cost efficiency. The commercial banking case provides an opportunity to examine this assumption more closely.

In sum, the data suggest that commercial banking reform conforms to three of the four assumptions about the causes and processes of change. The remaining sections of this chapter deepen and conclude the analysis. Section One addresses questions about economizing. Section Two integrates the analysis and examines incentives for change. Finally, Section Three draws lessons from the study to outline what we know and what we have yet to discover about the fundamental principles of economic and institutional change in commercial banking in the United States.

Economizing

The period 1960–2000 was one of the most intense periods of economic and institutional change in the banking industry in the 20th century with significant change beginning as early as 1965. Theoretically, these changes, which include an intensification of competition, technological change, and regulatory liberalization, ought to create incentives for banks to economize, resulting in substantial improvement in productivity. This section examines raw data that describes the behavior of costs over time, empirical studies of efficiency in banking, and changes in transaction costs.

Given the magnitude of change over the period 1960–2000, trend analysis will be more robust if it is based on a longer time series. Over the entire period 1934–2000, the expense of all commercial banking firms as a percentage of total income increased from 70% in 1934 to 76% in 2000. However, expenses were unusually high for most of the period 1965–1992. By 1965, total expense had increased to 75% of income, steadily increased to a high of 90% in 1981, and did not fall below 80% until 1992.

Total expense includes two types of expense, which banks account for separately: interest expense and non-interest expense. Interest expense, which includes total interest paid and accrued on all interest bearing liabilities, is a measure of the cost of funds. For most of the period covered by this study, the cost of funds is controlled in large part by policy making in the public sector, including interest rate adjustments and pricing regulation.[2] On the other hand, non-interest expense, which

[2] The components of interest expense include all interest expense on all liabilities reportable as deposits in domestic and foreign offices, the gross expenses of federal funds purchased and securities

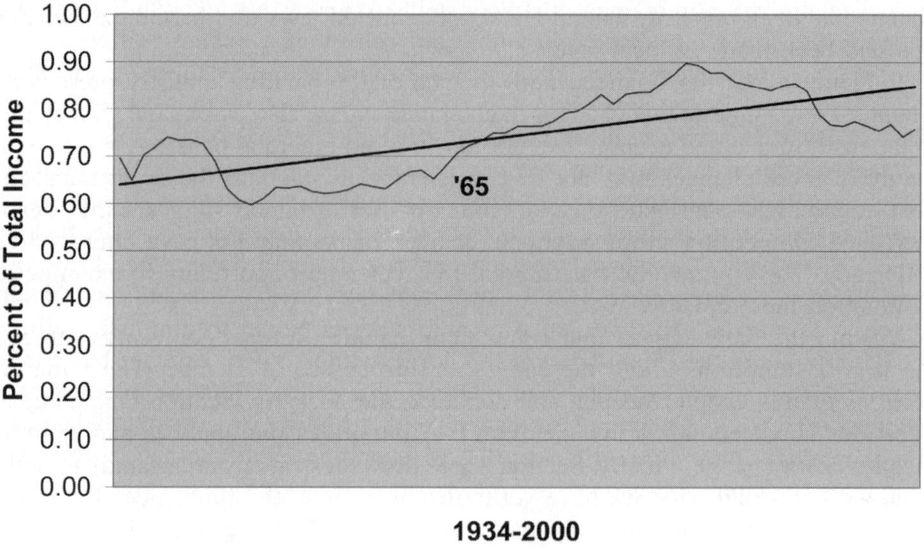

Figure 6.1. Total Expense.

Source: Author's estimate based on FDIC statistics.

includes employee salaries and benefits, occupancy expense, and other management expenses, reflects the costs of the way that banking firms choose to organize their activities.[3]

Decomposing total expense, interest expense as a percentage of total income increased from 19% in 1934 to 39% in 2000, whereas non-interest expense fell from 50% to 37%. Interest expense did not begin to increase until after 1961. In fact, it diminished after 1934 and remained stable over the period 1942–1955 at about 10% of total income. After 1955, it began to increase, reaching 19% of total income in 1960. After 1961, the rate of change quickened, and changes were more volatile. Interest expense reached 68% of total income in 1981, fell to 33% in 1993, and then stabilized at about 37% of income after 1995.

Non-interest expense increased after 1935 to 61% of total income in 1940, fell

---

sold, the interest expense related to demand notes issued to the U.S. Treasury, mortgage indebtedness, obligations under capitalized leases, and other borrowed money, and interest expense related to subordinated notes and debentures. Historically, banks derive a significant portion of their funding from low cost sources, such as equity issues or demand deposits: this is particularly true for retail banks. In 1997, the average rate paid on funds was 3.98% (Standard and Poor's, 1998).

[3] "Other" expense includes fees paid to directors, trustees and advisory board members, premiums on fidelity insurance and deposit insurance, retainer and legal fees, net losses from the sale or disposition of certain assets including those associated with acquisitions and mergers, management fees assessed by parent bank holding companies, advertising, public relations and promotion, amortization of intangible assets, charitable contributions, net losses on futures and forward contracts, charge-offs and write-downs of securities prior to sale, office supplies, information processing, telephone expenses, examination and audit fees, and other miscellaneous expenses.

to 52% in 1944, and remained relatively stable at about this level until 1960, when it began to further diminish. As is the case with interest expense, after 1960, the rate of change quickened and changes were more volatile. However, rather than increasing, non-interest expense fell to 22% of total income in 1981, increased to 44% in 1993, and then stabilized at about 40% after 1995.

Decomposition of non-interest expense shows that changes over the period are driven by salaries and benefits and "other" expense. In the post W.W. II period, occupancy expense fell to about 8.5% of total income, salaries and benefits increased to 61%, and "other" expense remained constant at about 35%. After 1960, occupancy expense increased to 16% of total non-interest expense and has remained stable at this level. However, salaries and benefits began to diminish, falling to 42% in 1992 and then stabilizing at this level, while "other" expense has continually increased to 47% of total non-interest expense in 2000. Augmented by the findings reported in Chapters Four and Five, this finding suggests that when banks did economize, they did so by substituting technology and alternative governance structures for labor and capital.

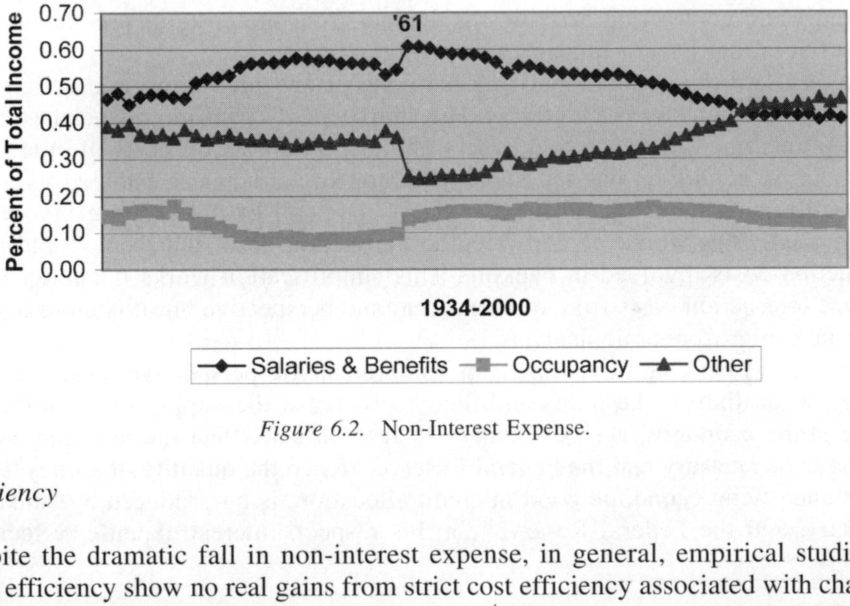

Figure 6.2. Non-Interest Expense.

Efficiency

Despite the dramatic fall in non-interest expense, in general, empirical studies of bank efficiency show no real gains from strict cost efficiency associated with changes in the economic and institutional environment.[4] However a recent study by Berger and Mester (2001), which combines several methods to capture potential improvements from cost, scale, and consumption economies over the period 1984–1997, finds that while cost productivity worsened over the period 1991–1997, profit productivity, which includes revenues as well as costs, improved dramatically. The

[4] See for example, Akhavein, Berger, and Humphrey (1997), Berger (1998), Hughes, Lang, Mester, and Moon (1996), Humphrey and Pulley (1997), Klein and Saidenberg (1998), and Pilloff and Santomero (1988). For overviews of the literature, see Berger and Mester (1997), Berger and Humphrey (1997), and Santomero and Eckles (2000).

authors' explanation for these findings is that banks are trying to maximize profits by increasing revenues as well as reducing costs. This can be accomplished by providing services that add higher value: e.g. by providing higher quality service, costs increase but revenues increase more than costs, which generates a net profit gain. In further analysis, Berger and Mester find that the behavior of banks involved in merger activity accounts for most of their findings: the cost productivity of merging banks was worse than for banks that did not engage in merger and acquisition activity, and profit productivity was better. In combination with raw expense data, these findings suggest that merger and acquisition activity in commercial banking has thus far produced profit efficiency but not strict cost efficiency.[5]

Transaction Costs

The theory of transaction cost economizing has been the subject of considerable debate, however, most scholars agree that transaction costs are important and a general consensus about the definition of the concept emerges from the literature.[6] Generally, transaction costs are the sum of the costs associated with engaging in exchange and contracting activities as distinct from the costs of producing goods and services that have a fundamental economic value.

Having said this, operationalizing the concept and measuring transaction costs in the banking industry is a bit tricky. The unique role of banks in financial exchange and contracting, which involves ameliorating the transaction costs of credit allocation in an economy, has led some scholars to characterize banking as a pure transaction cost industry.[7] From this perspective, all of the expense involved in banking activities would be construed as transaction costs and there would be no production costs involved in banking. This simplification works if one wishes to analyze transaction costs from a macroeconomic perspective but it is more troublesome in a microeconomic analysis.

Looking at banking activities from a microanalytic perspective, banks produce money when they make loans and thereby increase the supply of money circulating in the economy. The only other entities that can affect the monetary supply are the U.S. Treasury and the Federal Reserve. Hence the quantity of money, which is the underlying economic good in credit allocation, is co-produced by banks, the Treasury, and the Federal Reserve.[8] In this respect, interest expense reflects the

[5] Studies of the performance effects of mergers and acquisitions in banking also find limited evidence of strict cost efficiency gains. For an overview, see Rhoades (1994).

[6] For an overview of the literature and the debate, see Polski (2001).

[7] See for example, Wallis and North (1986). For a critique of this approach, see Davis (1986).

[8] Co-production refers to an economic situation in which both the consumer and the producer participate in producing the good or service. In the case of money, the Treasury prints money, the Federal Reserve sets the price of money, both buy and sell money but banks can also affect the quantity of money circulating in the economy through their lending and reserve activities. Other examples of co-produced goods and services include education and health: in both cases, the consumer must participate in the production regime in order to obtain benefits. For a discussion of the concept, see Ostrom, Schroeder, and Wynne (1993).

cost of producing money and may be construed as production costs, whereas non-interest expense, which reflects the costs of arranging transactions, may be construed as transaction costs.

When the behavior of both interest and non-interest expense is compared over time, an inverse relationship emerges. As interest expense diminishes after 1934, non-interest expense increases. Both types of expense are stable in the post W.W. II period. As interest expense increases in the late 1950s, non-interest expense diminishes. Both interest and non-interest expense converge to about 40% of total income in 1969 and maintain this level until 1973. Over the period 1973–1981, interest expense increases and non-interest expense diminishes. After 1981, both types of expense reverse direction and converge at about 40% of total income in 1992.

While the fall in non-interest expense from 50% of income in 1934 to 37% in 2000 suggests a tendency to minimize transaction costs over the long-term as Williamson theorizes, the data are ambiguous over the short and medium term. First, recall that banks began to make significant governance changes after 1965, yet non-interest expense began to diminish in the late 1950s before significant governance changes occurred. Over the period 1966–1971, banks were converting to the bank holding company form, which was a very significant change in governance, yet non-interest expense was stabilizing rather than diminishing. On the other hand, when non-interest expense began to diminish again over the period 1973–1981, banks were implementing transaction process innovations, re-engineering financial transactions, and embarking on a new wave of holding company formations, all of which involve adjusting governance mechanisms and are thus consistent with the theory of transaction cost economizing. However during the period in which banks were making governance changes by means of mergers and acquisitions (1981–1998), the ratio of ratio of non-interest expense to total income rose instead of fell and then stabilized at a level that was lower than it had been in 1934, but higher than it's most recent low point.

If we only look at "other" expense, the component of non-interest expense that is most directly related to governance, as governance changes were implemented,

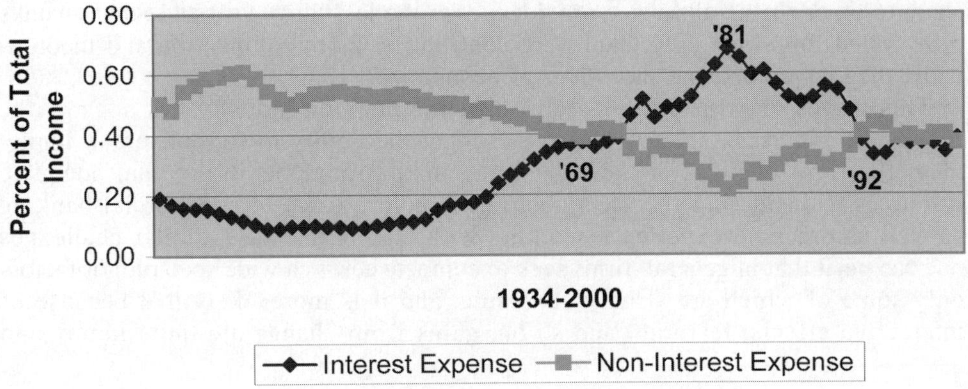

Figure 6.3. Interest and Non-Interest Expense.

costs consistently increased over the period 1960–2000 rather than decreased, which is inconsistent with the transaction cost economizing thesis. Finally, the inverse relationship between interest expense and non-interest expense over the period 1934–2000, suggests that there may be an interactive relationship between the two types of economizing. Assuming that this analysis is actually measuring transaction costs – and it may not – these findings have the following implications for the theory of transaction cost economizing: 1) a firm's motivation to adjust governance mechanisms may not involve strict cost efficiency, 2) firms may be motivated to economize but unable to do so perfectly, or 3) firms may be motivated to economize by reducing transaction costs and competent to do so, but the process of transaction cost economizing may be quite lumpy.

Summing up, despite extensive economic and institutional change, it is not clear that banks have economized as much as our theories suggest they ought. This finding may result from measurement problems: measuring economic behavior is difficult under static conditions but even more so under dynamic conditions and so it may be that we are not accurately differentiating between different types of costs or measuring efficiency gains. It may also indicate that bank managers did not believe that the competitive situation required them to economize, although this is unlikely given evidence on financial performance, innovation, and their testimony before Congress in hearings on reform.

Another possible explanation for relatively weak efforts to economize is that financial services markets are not as competitive as we believe them to be and have not provided adequate incentives for change. The support for this explanation is mixed. Banking still has a very large local component and local market concentration, which has always been high, has not significantly changed over time. Moreover, as state and national markets have become more important, concentration has been increasing at these levels. Coincident with economic and institutional change banking markets are becoming more concentrated and hence structure provides rather weak incentives for economizing. On the other hand, some research suggests that banks with persistently high profits are not consistently those with high market power.[9] Moreover, banks have lost significant market share to other financial service providers over the last thirty years and many banks have failed. In which case, banks are confronting more competition and theoretically, they have adequate incentives to economize.

This leaves us with the possibility that the banking industry has not met the pre-conditions necessary for adaptive change: the ability to formulate and implement the right changes at the right time, institutional flexibility, and adequate resources. Considering the facts about economic change in commercial banking as well as practical experience working with clients that face similar challenges one can posit that in general, firms seek to compete across a wide spectrum of factors only some of which are strictly economic, and it is more likely that because of interactive effects, learning, and so on, gains from change are quite lumpy and

---

[9] See Berger, Bonime, Covitz, and Hancock (2000). Also see Berger and Mester (2001) who reject the market power explanation for their findings of improved profit efficiency.

only realized after a significant lag. Both observations, neither of which are particularly new if viewed from the perspective of managerial economics, suggest that banks may not be as likely or as able to make change as we suppose, lacking necessity, ability, sufficient institutional flexibility, or resources. In short, not only do banks fail to conform to a fully rational economic model, the economic nature of banking and the preference functions of those who use the banking system may nevertheless permit banks to endure, which poses a further challenge to standard theory. In any case, it appears that the banking system has not provided sufficient incentives for banks to consistently economize, which means that there is more that bank managers can do to realize gains from the economic and institutional changes of the past thirty years, and more that regulators can do to encourage additional change.

Incentives to Change

The literature review in Chapter Two identifies three general perspectives with respect to incentives to engage in economic and institutional change.[10] From the social welfare perspective, cost efficiency is the primary incentive for change, from the distributional perspective, it is the opportunity of obtaining economic rents and political votes, and from the institutional perspective, it is transaction cost economizing. The facts of commercial banking reform challenge each of these perspectives. As financial services markets have become more competitive and banks have lost market power, they appear to have sought profit efficiency rather than either strict cost efficiency or pure rents. Moreover, a great deal of economic and institutional reform did not involve the political process, did not need to, and hence did not provide the opportunity for using the process to obtain rents or votes. Yet firms, regulators, and legislators were early and important participants in reform.

To be sure, it is naive to assume that when conditions change firms do not seek rents or that legislators do not opportunistically seek political support: firms need rents to compete over the long term and regulators and legislators need political support to meet their legal duties. Sometimes both firms and policy makers push the edges of the regulatory envelope too far or succumb to less than virtuous objectives.[11] But these assumptions are too general to provide insights that are powerful enough to inform experience or allow us to compare the adaptive capacity of one political economic system with another. A deeper dive into the specifics of commercial banking reform is required to understand of the true nature of the incentives of firms, regulators, and legislators to engage in economic and institutional change.

---

[10] See Chapter Two, Table 2.1, for a summary of these perspectives.

[11] The exploits of the S&Ls and the Keating Seven are illustrative, as are recent revelations about the involvement of some large banks in untoward financial dealings in the energy, telecom, and technology sectors.

Firms

In the U.S., commercial banks are neither strictly private nor wholly public sector entities. They are organized as private corporations and funded by private investors in either private or public capital markets. To obtain capital, they must deliver a competitive return on investment. Yet their activities are regulated in the public sector as well as by capital markets: they operate under either a federal or state charter, their liabilities to depositors are partially insured, and their activities are supervised by federal and state banking policymakers. Should they fail to meet regulatory requirements, they are subject to discipline, including closure. Hence banks are competitive in the U.S. if and only if they can satisfy both markets and governments.

In the 1960s, every aspect of the commercial banking business was regulated by a densely interwoven system of state, federal, and administrative law. While it was theoretically possible for firms outside the banking industry to compete with banks, the structure of the financial services industry and the structure of relative prices ceded competitive advantage to banks. A change in the relative prices of money and information processing in the 1970s reduced banks' competitive advantage and created incentives for firms outside the traditional banking industry to enter the industry by offering substitute products and services with equal or superior price-performance tradeoffs.

As competition increased and the banking industry's share of financial intermediary assets eroded, some banks embraced economic and institutional change whereas others actively resisted change. The contradictory response of banks to changing conditions in the industry has been attributed to a largely irrational populist contest between large and small banks that is rooted in the historical tension between country banks and city banks. However, this explanation cannot account for the remarkably broad and historically novel consensus for reform that emerged over time. A more likely alternative explanation is that the combination of changing economic and institutional conditions and the fragmented structure of the U.S. commercial banking industry creates very different incentives for growth and change. Banks with governance structures that do not demand aggressive profit growth or that operate in protected markets with few growth prospects have limited incentives to invest in change. On the other hand, banks with growth-oriented governance structures have greater incentives to seek reform as do those banks that operate in competitive markets and are forced to change to survive. As conditions change and more banks are threatened or acquired by larger, more aggressively growth-oriented holding companies, the incentives of banks to engage in reform change.

For example, members of the Independent Bankers Association (IBA), which are typically banks in small communities that operate in highly protected markets, opposed reform. From their perspective, reform was either unnecessary or a threat; hence they had little incentive to pursue change strategies. Conversely, many members of the American Bankers' Association (ABA), which tend to be larger, publicly owned banks operating in urban areas that face more competitive conditions, actively sought reform because they viewed it as a means to survive and grow.

Until conditions changed in the 1970s, the number of *status quo* oriented banks exceeded the number of change oriented banks. In the 1970s, as more banks became part of larger, growth oriented holding companies, banks changed type, which favored the formation of political coalitions for change. Rather than being a cause of change as distributional theorists posit, successful political coalition formation emerged as a consequence of the metamorphosis of *status quo* oriented banks into change-oriented banks.[12] This transformation is largely due to changes in the identity and governance structure of banks, which was an adaptive response to changes in competitive conditions.

In sum, the structure of the U.S. commercial banking industry is such that some banks have greater incentives to compete in ways that are consistent with standard theory than others: variations in market conditions and governance structure may account for the difference. Managers who opportunistically reorganized banks under holding companies umbrellas not only side-stepped regulatory constraints on powers and acquired new incentives for growth and change, they acquired new capital and tax tools that have facilitated aggressive diversification and expansion. Regulators and policy makers augmented these incentives by linking capital structure and powers as well as by encouraging consolidation. However, these linkages, which regulators and policy makers have assumed will induce more prudent and economically efficient bank management, also create incentives to make mergers and acquisitions and engage in financial engineering that increases the volume of off-balance sheet activities.

At present, it is an open question whether the combination of merger and acquisition activity, consolidation, and financial engineering has created adequate managerial incentives to improve the economics of banking, lower risk, improve performance, or protect the overall stability of the commercial banking system. The data on economizing suggest that this combination may allow banks to build financial scale and scope while avoiding more difficult, fundamental change. Consistent with Schumpeter's assumptions about the nature of incentives to compete, changing competitive conditions may stimulate firms to preserve a way of doing business rather than to *per se* economize. In which case, we cannot assume that stimulating competition will always clear markets: instead, it may create new sources of rigidity and new coordination risks.

Regulators

U.S. bank regulators have a legal duty to regulate banks in a way that preserves the safety and soundness of the financial system. They provide information and advice to legislators and the public about regulatory control and monitor and enforce existing law. Much to the dissatisfaction of some banking economists, they are also empowered to exercise discretion in approving changes in the activities of banking firms. While regulators do not have a *per se* duty to protect the competi-

[12] For an interesting perspective on the evolution of political coalition formation in the industry, see Yingling (1994).

tiveness of the banking industry or prevent losses from bank failures, as business conditions change, they do have a duty to assure that the response to these changes does not impair safe asset transformation and credit allocation. While the structure of their authority permits them to operate on a proactive as well as reactive basis, they do not have unilateral powers: their actions and decisions are subject to challenge in legislatures and in the courts.

It is often argued in the banking literature that the fragmented structure of regulatory authority prevents regulators from fulfilling their duty by inhibiting effective coordination and making it easy to evade responsibility for action. To be sure, we can find anecdotes that support this proposition; however in a systematic analysis, the commercial banking case does not confirm it. Regulators were very active participants in banking reform, analyzing banking conditions, exercising considerable discretionary authority when the banking system was financially troubled, managing a volume of assistance transactions that has not been seen since the Great Depression, and formulating policy recommendations. While the Board of Governors of the Federal Reserve, the FDIC, the OCC, and state regulators have not and do no always agree they nevertheless coordinated rather closely to advance commercial banking reform, protect depositors, and preserve stability. But why might this be?

Regulators first engaged in banking reform when banks began to reorganize under holding company umbrellas, which coincides with changing economic conditions in the industry. As financial conditions worsened in the industry in the 1980s and 1990s, regulators became increasingly involved in reform. Recall that the deposits of most U.S. commercial banks are insured by the FDIC. While banks pay premiums to fund the FDIC, if bank failures exceed the resources of the fund, the U.S. Treasury stands as the lender of last resort. As competition took its toll and financial conditions deteriorated in the industry, the deposit insurance fund came under increasing pressure, which created strong incentives for regulators to pursue reform.

Standard approaches to deposit insurance take a rather narrow view of the lender of last resort rule.[13] In the classic conceptualization, the activity of transforming liquid liabilities (deposits) into illiquid assets (loans) creates a time inconsistency risk that poses a fundamental but unavoidable threat to systemic stability. Deposit insurance, which is conceptualized as a trilateral performance bond in which an insurance agency provides a bond that protects depositors, solves this problem by sustaining depositor confidence in the banking system and thereby avoiding runs and panics. However, it is typically assumed that deposit insurance creates moral hazard by making it possible for banks to raise funds for risky projects at costs that do not adequately reflect the risk of the project. Moreover, it is assumed that deposit insurance encourages depositors to neglect monitoring banks, thereby inhibiting the smooth functioning of market mechanisms. Regulators are believed to lack incentives to enforce loss-control measures because of conflicting incentives among bank owners, managers, regulators, legislators, and government officials.

---

[13] For overviews of the literature, see Bhattacharya and Thakor (1993), Santomero (1997) and FDIC (1997). Diamond and Dybvig (1983) provide the classic statement of the deposit insurance problem.

While standard critiques of deposit insurance provide intuitively appealing theoretical arguments, they have limited empirical support, generate incomplete models of bank regulation, and overlook the adaptive aspects of the lender of last resort rule. The history of banking is rife with examples of excessive risk taking long before deposit insurance was implemented and at a time when markets were the primary source of regulation in the banking system. While one might quibble about what might have been done to prevent the banking crises of the 1980s and early 1990s or to mitigate the extent of the damage, whether incentives conflicted or not, a remarkably diverse set of regulators in the public and private sectors coordinated to enforce sufficient loss control measures to protect both depositors and bank investors, and maintain systemic stability.

More concretely, the U.S. is a very large, diverse, and integrated political economy with a polycentric structure in which local control is the norm. In this political economic context, another way to think about the lender of last resort rule is as a relatively noninvasive extra-market coordination mechanism that operates only when intervention is required at the systemic level. As 19th century experience demonstrates, a wholly market driven banking system is quite unstable, posing a threat to local, regional, and national economic stability and growth. The lender of last resort rule creates conditional interdependency among otherwise independent actors: a negative change in the financial condition of the banking industry aligns incentives to identify and solve the problems associated with financial distress.

In financial terms, the lender of last resort rule makes non-financial businesses, other taxpayers, and governments contingent bondholders in banks. Contingent public liability creates a formidable regulatory wedge of public and private investors that both protects private interest in obtaining a competitive return on investment and public interest in preserving the systemic stability that is essential for sustained capital accumulation and investment. The wedge includes private equity investors, private bondholders, and contingent public bondholders. Each group has fiduciaries who are obligated under civil and criminal law to protect their interests. Private investors are represented by the officers and directors of the Board of Directors of the bank, and contingent public investors are represented by regulators, the Board of Governors of the Federal Reserve, and the Secretary of the Treasury.

In sum, there is no question that banking regulation is quite fragmented in the U.S. – this study shows that it is even more fragmented than it is typically conceived to be. However, contrary to conventional wisdom, this fragmentation does not necessarily imply that regulators do not have sufficient incentives to impose effective loss control measures. While reasonable people may disagree about the precise level of acceptable loss limits, commercial banking reform demonstrates that properly conceived, the current regulatory structure provides strong incentives to coordinate to assure that the banking industry is both commercially viable and systemically sound. Moreover, we have little to fear and much to gain from regulatory discretion providing that it is embedded in a set of institutional arrangements that places checks and balances on conflicting interests.

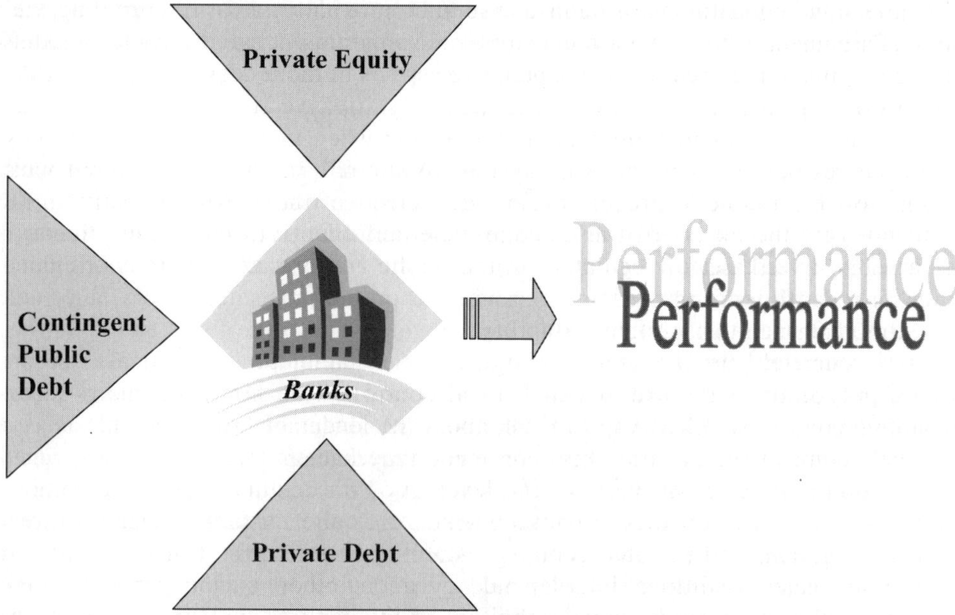

Figure 6.4. The Regulatory Wedge.

Legislators

In U.S. state and federal governments, legislators have a duty to represent the constituents who elect them to office and to uphold the Constitution of the government in which they participate. They meet this duty by investigating the need for policy reform, writing new laws, persuading their constituents and colleagues of the value of their policy solutions, and negotiating compromises that satisfy conflicting demands and evolving needs.[14] Like regulators, they do not have unilateral powers: public policy is subject to veto by governing executives and can be challenged in the courts. If legislators fail to meet their duty, they may be sanctioned or removed from office. With respect to banking regulation, a dual system gives jurisdiction over state chartered banks and interstate banking activities to state legislators and governors, and jurisdiction over nationally chartered banks and national banking law to federal legislators and the President.

While scholars working in the distributional political economy tradition posit that legislators respond to the opportunity to collect votes (or avoid losing votes), and institutional political economists assume that legislators respond to changes in transaction costs, the pattern of change in U.S. commercial banking suggests an alternative explanation that is more consistent with the structure of the U.S. polit-

[14] For a description and analysis of the legislative process as it pertains to banking reform, see Polski (1997).

ical economy: legislators have an incentive to initiate policy reform when it appears that it is necessary to do so either because constituents demand change or effective government requires it. As Chapter Five argues in more detail, the institutional structure of government in the United States mitigates against both wholesale opportunism and bureaucratic control.

In the case of commercial banking reform, which had bipartisan support, both incentives operated: constituent demand and effective government. Recall that the structure of political control and economic development in the United States is both decentralized and polycentric. From the earliest days of the Republic, the states and the federal government have depended upon a combination of local private and public finance to facilitate growth and development. Like firms and countries, states within the United States compete with each other for investment. Because banks provide finance for individual, business, and government investment, access to strong banks provides a state with a competitive advantage. Yet since the late 19th century, local and regional economies have become increasingly integrated and financial contagion is more likely. Economic integration creates interdependency among banks, non-financial businesses, governments, and labor, which in turn, creates a common interest in financial stability. The interdependency that arises from private economic activity is further strengthened by the system of funds transfers between states and the federal government that has evolved over the course of the 20th century.

The importance of financial services in the U.S. economy is demonstrated in part by statistics on industry Gross State Product (GSP). Looking at figures for 1987, a year that coincides with interstate banking reform, the finance, insurance and real estate industry (FIRE) accounted for nearly one fifth of GSP. At the regional level, the industry contributed from 16.4% of GSP to 23.3%. When private interests and public interests overlap as extensively as they do in the case of financial services, it is exceedingly difficult to characterize the motivations of legislators who engage in the process of reform or to locate them on a uni-dimensional scale.

Table 6.1. Percent of Real Gross State Product in Finance, Insurance, and Real Estate in 1987

Region	% GSP
United States	19.3
Mideast	23.3
New England	22.9
Far West	21.6
Great Lakes	16.9
Rocky Mountain	16.9
Plains	16.7
Southwest	16.5
Southeast	16.4

Source: Beemiller and Woodruff III (2000).

Lessons

This study addresses a very complex problem in political economy: institutional change in a large scale polycentric system that produces and regulates a quasi-public good. By definition, a polycentric system has no single source of authority or coercive power. It has no leviathan to impose its will and no neutral social planner to discover and implement social optima. Instead, heterogeneous actors operating in a fragmented system must coordinate to overcome collective action problems to realize their diverse objectives. The commercial bank reform case demonstrates that as Mancur Olson has observed, collective action problems cannot be solved in large heterogeneous groups without the aid of "special institutions."[15] And so in many respects, the lessons we can most usefully draw from this study pertain to the nature of the special coordinating institutions that made it possible for the commercial banking industry to deviate from a well-established path.

In general, commercial banking reform arose as a function of changes in beliefs, governance, and economizing, which were stimulated by economic and institutional shocks that altered business opportunities. External shocks interacted with institutional arrangements to create interdependency among actors in the private and public sectors, which created incentives to engage in reform. Reform was mediated by a more extensive set of arrangements that provided a means to discover collective interests, engage in joint problem solving, and evolve and change in an orderly fashion. In other words, it was the structure of the banking system and the governance system within which it is embedded that shaped adaptation and innovation. Responses were a function of other sets of institutional arrangements that structured the effects of change and the patterns of interaction among the participants. None of which suggests that coordination was optimal, only that at a particular moment in time, the intersection of economic conditions and governance mechanisms created incentives to coordinate to solve individual and joint problems.

From this general lesson, we can extract the following implications for managing adaptive change in the U.S. commercial banking system:

- Both economic conditions and institutions matter and policymakers need to be alert to the interactive effects of economic change and policy change. How economic conditions and institutions matter depends upon the nature of changing conditions and the extent to which existing economic and institutional structures provide incentives to adapt to external change in ways that are consistent with stable growth and development. While external shocks present an opportunity for new growth and development as well as a threat to the existing economic order, an evolutionary perspective is required to understand the path of change and the impact of potential policy interventions. To this end, there is need for further research in evolutionary economics.[16] Moreover, there is a need for microanalytic studies of market clearing. The banking reform case provides additional

[15] Olson (1965).

[16] For a starting point, see Nelson (1996).

support for the notion that price changes interact with governance structure. If either governance structure or market structure interferes with market clearing, the incentive for reform at the operating level will be distorted, which will distort collective action. This implies that a change in relative prices is a necessary but not a sufficient condition for structural reform.

- Developing a better understanding of the types of institutions that are instrumental in market clearing requires a better understanding of personal motivation and the nature of competition. This study finds that considerable individual and collective capital was invested in reform yet there is only partial support for standard explanations of the motivation for this involvement, including the theory of transaction cost economizing. While there is an extensive literature that critiques standard conceptions of rationality and self-interest, few alternative theories have been articulated and tested in different governance systems.[17] A regulatory wedge consisting of private equity investors, private debt holders, and contingent public debt holders appears to govern commercial banking activities, yet we know very little about how this wedge influences the motivations of different types of participants under different sets of conditions. Finally, there is much to be learned about the adaptive characteristics and innovative capacity of firms, regulators, and policymakers.
- U.S. commercial banking is not wholly regulated by markets or governments: it is regulated by a deeply integrated combination of market-based coordination mechanisms, government authority, and policy instruments. Scholarship on comparative economic systems has a tendency to draw an artificial dichotomy among these regulatory devices and to strictly characterize a particular system as dominated by one or the other, which leads to overly general observations and naïve policy prescriptions. Progress in comparative research will require deeper analyses of the nature of regulatory mechanisms, the economic and governance context within which they are embedded, and the adaptive performance of these systems when conditions change. In the U.S. context, there is more to be learned by examining theoretically the characteristics of deposit guarantees and regulatory discretion as coordinating mechanisms in large scale adaptive change. The regional banking compact is another very interesting solution to coordination that should be examined theoretically.
- A broader and arguably more important research agenda relates to understanding and comparing the dynamics of polycentric systems.[18] As originally formulated by V. Ostrom, Tiebout, and Warren (1961), polycentric governance is a compromise between hierarchical governance, which has extensive information problems and distorted incentives for individual initiative, and anarchy, which cannot provide the fundamental certainty required for sustained social commit-

---

[17] For a very interesting exception, see Frey (1997) who develops an alternative theory of personal motivation. For an overview of the issues and results obtained in experimental economics, see Camerer (1998) and Fehr and Schmidt (1998).

[18] For a very thoughtful essay on the theoretical underpinnings and research implications of the concept of polycentricity, see V. Ostrom (1972).

ment. Most of us have been trained to think about and order the social world in hierarchical terms. However, it may be that there are more polycentric orders in the naturally occurring world than hierarchical orders, if for no other reason than that all systems leak and these leaks can erode formal authority structures.[19] Yet we know very little about the coordinating mechanisms that make it possible to resolve tensions between specific and common interests in polycentric systems. Hence the very concept of polycentricity poses critical and very fundamental questions of political, economic, and institutional theory.

In summary, this study challenges a number of standard assumptions about the nature of the U.S. commercial banking system and the political economy of economic and regulatory change. It offers an alternative framework for analyzing regulatory systems in the U.S., provides a general theory of change, and reframes the debate about banking regulation. Findings regarding the causes and processes of change raise many new questions. Hopefully these questions are sufficiently compelling to capture and hold the imagination of a generation or more of scholars of political economy, as well as to provide a whole new class of solutions to age-old problems of economic growth and change.

---

[19] In addition to federalist governance systems, regional governance systems, and international governance systems, good examples of the potential for polycentric orders are suggested by the existence of parallel political and economic systems in many developing countries, the emergence of "outlaw" societies in totalitarian regimes, the networks and other informal organizational orders that emerge to cure coordination failures such as those that exist as a function of technological change or unmitigated diseconomies of scale in hierarchical organizations.

EPILOGUE

The Future of U.S. Commercial Banking

As restrictions on scope and powers were eased in the 1980s, banks morphed into a new kind of financial services entity. The modern U.S. bank is no longer a commercial bank, an investment bank, or a merchant bank. Its main activities involve managing and financing mergers, acquisitions, and divestitures; financing equipment leasing; financing the expansion of businesses; providing cash and transaction management services; and asset management. For many of the top global firms, an increasingly greater share of income comes from trading for their own account as well as with each other, and less from fees that clients pay for services. And some traditional client services are effectively subsidized by cash and asset management services.

The effects of industry reforms are reflected in financial performance after 1993, when banks reported improvements in asset growth, cost structures, profits, and capital adequacy, and the number of problem institutions declined. Robust stock prices and excess capital levels created favorable conditions for continued growth in merger and acquisition activity, resulting in further consolidation in the industry. Diversification reduced banks' vulnerability to downturns in particular regions and in specialized business lines. In 1999, just prior to entering the recession, industry earnings increased at the rate of 16% year to year, delivering a record Return on Assets of 1.31%.

However, despite record levels of profitability at the turn of the 20th century, in recent periods, higher loan loss provision expenses and narrowing net interest margins have created new pressures on bank profitability. While U.S. banks entered the recession in a strong position with better capital and reserve positions than they had in the 1980s and early 1990s, the recent downturn in the U.S. economy as well as the lending excesses of the 1990s will take their toll. In the first two years of the 21st century there has been a pronounced increase in non-performing assets, particularly at large banks, a rapid deterioration of credit quality in certain segments of bank portfolios – most notably within the corporate loan book – and meager growth in retail core deposits. In combination, these developments create pressure on bank liquidity: benchmark ratios such as loans-to-deposits are at historic peaks. Results for year ending December 31, 2001 reflect these vulnerabilities. The FDIC reports that in the 4th quarter of 2001, net charge-offs for the 25 largest U.S. banks increased 64% over the prior year and non-performing assets increased

25%. As corporate scandals continue to unfold, it is clear that bankruptcies and debt defaults will be a continuing problem. Noting well the lessons of the 1970s and 1980s, the Chairman of the Federal Reserve has warned Congress that traditional measures of capital adequacy are less meaningful given the nature and complexity of risk undertaken by larger banking organizations in recent years.

Future Challenges

Have commercial banks survived the final decades of the 20th century only to disappear in the 21st century? It is too soon to answer this question but one thing is clear: pressure for change will not dissipate and it will be up to a new generation of bank managers and regulators to meet the challenge. The same fundamental forces that drove change in U.S. financial services markets in the late 20th century will operate in the 21st century: population demographics, the nature of economic activity, and technology. Individuals, businesses, governments and other institutional investors, who must finance the retirement of the aging baby boom population, will continue to exercise considerable impact on the supply of investment capital.

On the demand side, the economies of the "rust belt," which have yet to fully restructure to reflect the changing terms of trade in industrial and manufacturing goods and services, will require significant capital investment to be competitive in the 21st century. Continued expansion of local and cross-border economic activity will stimulate demand for new financial products, new services, new organizational structures, and new regulation. Extracting economic value from new discoveries in the life and materials sciences, which is a strategic focus for many local economic development initiatives, will feed demand for capital and the supply of capital. Finally, the process of applying the research that forms the foundation of these discoveries will lead to new technological innovations, which will further stimulate the demand and supply of capital as well as influence conduct, structure, and performance in financial services markets.

One of the key lessons we can take from thirty years of change in the commercial banking industry is that the prosperity of the industry will depend upon the quality of industry leadership and the wisdom of regulators. The extensiveness and complexity of banking regulation is a favorite scapegoat for performance problems in the U.S. banking industry. Many experts contend that "politics" inhibit competitiveness and growth in the banking sector. They argue that it is difficult to summon the political will to change existing regulations or to agree to new regulations when economic conditions change. Yet as this study demonstrates, the evidence for this proposition is rather sparse. Instead, detailed analysis of the period 1960–2000 suggests that there is considerable latitude in the U.S. banking system for change but it is bank managers and regulators rather than legislators who must lead.

As economic change reconfigured the competitive landscape in the late 20th century, creative bank managers pushed the edges of the regulatory envelope to reformulate the banking business. While legislators facilitated discussion and debate about reform, change was initiated and implemented by pro-active firms and knowledgeable regulators. Many (but not all) banking firms and regulators took action before the legal framework for banking changed and before the direction of change was certain despite the potential for failure or a disabling challenge. Following the industry's lead, regulators relaxed restrictions for well capitalized banks and legislators reformed deeply entrenched rules that impaired macroeconomic competitiveness and growth.

In the years ahead, bank managers and regulators must lead new reform efforts because government cannot. Legislators are constrained by the activities of other policy makers particularly in areas related to trade, antitrust, and macroeconomic policy. These other types of policy making activities are not controlled by U.S. bank regulators, the banking industry, or banking concerns: they emerge from the interactions of multiple, separate, and often conflicting political and economic interests and forces. In addition, the interactive effects of disparate but related policies are not always obvious to policy makers. Even when these effects are apparent, policy makers cannot always coordinate effectively to reconcile conflicts. Both effects are exacerbated by innovation, which generates unpredictable consequences that are not only difficult to anticipate, but virtually impossible to regulate on a pre-emptive basis.

The increasingly international character of banking activities magnifies bank management and governance issues. Participation in the international financial system is not limited to global banks – the nature of modern economic life and hence modern banking dictates that every bank in the U.S. participates in the international financial system to some extent. International financial activity exposes U.S. banks to risks in every region of the world. Just as activities of individual banks within a domestic banking system have externalities, so too do the activities of individual banks within the international system. Difficult as it is to monitor risk in a domestic system, which has relatively familiar parameters, it is even more challenging to make this estimate for other country systems. Moreover, unlike the U.S. system, in which federal deposit guarantees act as a coordinating mechanism for large-scale change, no such mechanism currently exists in the international financial system.

Over the coming decades, bank managers and regulators will have to address the following challenges:

- Convergence among large, global banks will continue but banking systems will retain their distinctiveness at the country level. Nevertheless, banking systems in the advanced economies will continue to restructure. Hence global banks will have to become adept at operating in very different financial systems that are undergoing significant change. And domestic banks will have to anticipate and stay ahead of structural change in their own countries.
- More and more banking services are becoming commodities, hence banks will experience continuing pressure to reduce costs and focus on value-added products and services. These pressures will stimulate continued consolidation, a new focus on separating production and distribution activities, and innovations that elec-

tronically enable financial activity. It will be imperative that banks learn how to obtain value from mergers and acquisitions and to work effectively with strategic partners.

- Eventually there will be a face-off between insurance companies and banks based on their core competencies as financial intermediaries. Because insurance activities are regulated at the state level in the U.S., the process of change is likely to be similar to that of interstate banking reform.
- While U.S. banks now have the freedom to engage in universal banking, those that chose to do so will have to develop new business models that overcome the limitations of the traditional universal banking model.
- Banks will be forced to increase their innovative capacity. While some banks have demonstrated the ability to innovate in the areas of organizational design, process management, and financial engineering, banks lag other financial service providers in new product development. Moreover, there is much more that banks could do to improve profit and cost efficiency. However, success will require fundamental organizational transformation that is closely aligned to a clearly articulated business and technology strategy.
- Managing operational, systems, market, credit, regulatory, human resources, strategic, third party, and e-business risk will make or break a bank. Recent economic events are harbingers of the need to better anticipate and monitor domestic and overseas exposure and grapple with accounting transparency for off-balance sheet activities and investment concentrations in retirement plans. Capital adequacy will be an ongoing concern.
- Systemic risk arising from economic change, structural shifts in the banking and insurance industries, and the complex risk exposures created by financial innovations will be a continuing and worrisome threat to individual banks as well as domestic and global economic order. For example, the size of the inter-bank loan market for developed countries alone increased from $25 billion in 1999 to $662 billion in 2000, and the value of all cross border financial claims increased from $276 billion to over $1 trillion, yet banking experts and regulators do not fully understand the complex chain of financial flows and credit interdependencies in this market nor are they prepared to cope with a systemic crisis.
- Pressure to create an integrated international financial system that can work closely with domestic financial systems will intensify. This means that financial executives must work with domestic and international financial regulators on a pro-active basis in designing and implementing regulation that will protect the economic value of financial intermediation, assure the integrity and stability of financial markets, and maintain systemic stability.

References

Abramovitz, Moses. 1993. "The Search for the Sources of Growth: Areas of Ignorance, Old and New. *Journal of Economic History* **53**(2): 217–243.

Abrams, Burton A. and Russell F. Settle. 1993. "Pressure-group Influence and Institutional Change: Branch-Banking Legislation During the Great Depression." *Public Choice* **77**: 687–705.

Akhavein, Jalal D., Allen N. Berger, and David B. Humphrey. 1997. "The Effects of Megamergers on Efficiency and Prices: Evidence from a Bank Profit Function." *Review of Industrial Organization* **12**.

Allen, Franklin and Douglas Gale. 2001. *Comparative Financial Systems: A Survey.* Wharton Financial Institutions Working Paper. The Wharton School, University of Pennsylvania, April.

Allen, Franklin, James McAndrews, and Philip Strahan. 2001. *E-Finance: An Introduction.* Wharton Financial Institutions Working Paper 01-36. The Wharton School, University of Pennsylvania, October 7.

Alston, Lee J., Thráinn Eggertsson, and Douglass C. North. 1996. *Empirical Studies in Institutional Change.* New York, NY: Cambridge University Press.

Arrow, Kenneth. 1951. *Social Choice and Individual Values.* New York, NY: John Wiley & Sons, Inc.

Association of Registered Bank Holding Companies. 1973. "The Bank Holding Company: Its History and Significance in Modern America." Washington, D.C.

Baer, Herbert and Sue F. Gregorash (eds.). 1986. *Toward Nationwide Banking: A Guide To The Issues.* Chicago, IL: Federal Reserve Bank of Chicago.

Banning, Lance. 1995. *The Sacred Fire of Liberty: James Madison and the Founding of the Federal Republic.* Ithaca, NY: Cornell University Press.

Bates, Robert H., Avner Greif, Margaret Levi, Jean-Laurent Rosenthal, and Barry R. Weingast. 1998. *Analytic Narratives.* Princeton, NJ: Princeton University Press.

Beemiller, Richard M. and Clifford H. Woodruff III. 2000. "Gross State Product by Industry, 1977-98." *Survey of Current Business.* 69–90. October. Washington, D.C.: Bureau of Economic Analysis.

Benston, George J. 1986. "Federal Regulation of Banking: Historical Overview." In George G. Kaufman and R.C. Kormendt (eds.), *Deregulating Financial Services: Public Policy in Flux.* Cambridge, MA: Ballinger Publishing Company.

_____ (ed.). 1983. *Financial Services: The Changing Institutions and Government Policy.* Englewood Cliffs, NJ: Prentice-Hall, Inc.

Becker, Gary S. 1983. "A Theory of Competition among Pressure Groups For Political Influence." *Quarterly Journal of Economics* **XCVIII**(3), August.

Berger, Allen N. 1998. "The Efficiency Effects of Bank Mergers and Acquisitions: A Preliminary Look at the 1990s Data." In Amihud, Y. and G. Miller (eds.), *Bak Mergers and Acquisitions.* MA: Boston. Kluwer Academic Publishers.

Berger, A.N., S.D. Bonime, D.M. Corvitz, and D. Hancock. 2000. "Why Are Bank Profits So Persistent? The Roles of Product Market Competition, Informational Opacity, and Regional Macroeconomic Shocks." *Journal of Banking and Finance* **24**: 1203–1235.

Berger, Allen N., Rebecca S. Demsetz, and Philip E. Strahan. 1998. "The Consolidation of the Financial Service Industry: Causes, Consequences, and Implications for the Future." Mimeo, November.

Berger, Allen N. and David B. Humphrey. 1997. "Efficiency of Financial Institutions: International Survey and Directions for Future Research." Finance and Economics Discussion Series. Divisions of Research & Statistics and Monetary Affairs. Federal Reserve Board, Washington, D.C. January.

Berger, Allen N., Anil K. Kashyap, and Joseph M. Scalise. 1995. "The Transformation of the U.S. Banking Industry: What a Long, Strange Trip It's Been." *Brookings Papers on Economic Activity* **2**: 55–218.

Berger, Allen N. and Loretta J. Mester. 2001. "Explaining the Dramatic Changes in Performance of U.S. Banks: Technological Change, Deregulation, and Dynamic Changes in Competition." Wharton Financial Institutions Center Working Paper 01-22. Wharton School. University of Pennsylvania. April.

_____. 1997. "Inside the Black Box: What Explains Differences in the Efficiencies of Financial Institutions?" *Journal of Banking & Finance* **21**: 895–947.

Bernstein, Marver. 1955. *Regulating Business by Independent Commission*. Princeton, N.J.: Princeton University Press.

Bhattacharya, Sudipto and Anjan V. Thakor. 1993. "Contemporary Banking Theory." *Journal of Financial Intermediation* **3**: 2–50.

Biggar, Stephen. 2001. *Standard & Poor's Banking Industry Survey*. New York, NY, May 3.

Black, Duncan. 1958. *The Theory of Committees and Elections*. Cambridge, U.K.: Cambridge University Press.

Board of Governors of the Federal Reserve System. 1994. *The Federal Reserve System: Purposes & Functions*. Washington, D.C.

_____. 1978. "The Bank Holding Company Movement to 1978: A Compendium." Staff Study. Washington, D.C.

_____. 1960–2000. *Annual Report*. Washington, D.C.

_____. 1941–1970. Banking and Monetary Statistics. Washington, D.C.

Board on Science, Technology, and Economic Policy and the National Research Council. 1999. Securing *America's Industrial Strength*. Washington, D.C.: National Academy Press.

Boczar, Gregory E. 1975. "The Growth of Multi-bank Holding Companies: 1956–1973." Staff Study. Washington, D.C.: Board of Governors of the Federal Reserve.

Boyd, John H. and Mark Gertler. 1993. "U.S. Commercial Banking: Trends, Cycles, and Policy." Working Paper No. 4404. National Bureau of Economic Research. Cambridge, MA.

Breyer, Stephen. 1982. *Regulation and Its Reform*. Cambridge, MA: Harvard University Press.

Buchanan, James M. and Gordon Tullock. 1962. *The Calculus of Consent: Logical Foundations of Constitutional Democracy*. Ann Arbor, MI: University of Michigan Press.

Calomiris, Charles W. 1993. "Regulation, Industrial Structure, and Instability in U.S. Banking: An Historical Perspective." In Klausner, Michael and Lawrence J. White (eds.), *Structural Change in Banking*. Homewood, IL: Business One Irwin.

Calomiris, Charles W. and Eugene N. White. 1994. "The Origins of Federal Deposit Insurance." In Claudia Golden and Gary Libecap (eds.), *The Regulated Economy: A Historical Approach to Political Economy*. A National Bureau of Economics Research Project Report.

Camerer, Colin. 1998. "Bounded Rationality in Individual Decision Making." *Experimental Economics* **1**(2): 163–183.

Carlton, Dennis W. 1989. "The Theory and the Facts of How Markets Clear: Is Industrial Organization Valuable for Understanding Macroeconomics?" In Richard Schmalensee and Robert Willig (eds.), *Handbook of Industrial of Industrial Organization*. Volume II. Amsterdam, The Netherlands: North-Holland.

Clark, Robert C. 1983. "Agency Costs versus Fiduciary Duties." In *Asymmetric Information, the Agency Problem and Modern Business Practice*. Harvard Business School 75th Anniversary Colloquium, June 20–23.

Coase, Ronald J. 1960. "The Problem of Social Cost," *Journal of Law and Economics* **I**.

_____. 1937. "The Nature of the Firm," *Economica*, New Series, Vol. **IV**, 1937, reprinted in American Economic Association. 1952. Stigler, G.J. and Boulding, K.E. (eds.), *Readings in Price Theory*. Irwin.

Commons, John R. 1968. *Legal Foundations of Capitalism.* Madison, WI: University of Wisconsin Press.

Conference of State Bank Supervisors. 1996. *Profile of State Chartered Banking.* Washington, D.C.

Cooke, Jacob E. (ed.). 1961. *The Federalist.* Middletown: Wesleyan University Press.

Corigan, E. Gerald. 1982. "Are Banks Special?" *Federal Reserve Bank of Minneapolis Annual Report.*

Crandall, Robert W. 1991. *After the Breakup: U.S. Telecommunications in a More Competitive Era.* Washington, D.C.: The Brookings Institution.

Dahl, Robert A. and Charles E. Lindblom. 1953. *Politics, Economics, and Welfare.* New York, NY:Harper and Row.

Davis, Lance E. 1986. "Comment on Measuring the Transaction Sector in the American Economy." In Stanley L Engerman and Robert E. Gallman (eds.), *Longterm Factors in American Economic Growth.* Volume 51 of Studies in Income and Wealth Series. Chicago, IL: University of Chicago Press.

Derthick, Martha and Paul J. Quirk. 1985. *The Politics of Regulation.* Washington, D.C.: Brookings Institution.

Diamond, D.W. and P. Dybvig. 1983. "Bank Runs, Deposit Insurance, and Liquidity." *Journal of Political Economy* **91**: 401–419.

Dixit, Avinash. 1996. *The Making of Economic Policy: A Transaction-Cost Politics Perspective.* Cambridge: MIT Press.

Downs, Anthony. 1957. *An Economic Theory of Democracy.* New York, NY: Harper & Row.

Drucker, Peter. 1999. "Innovate or Die." *The Economist*, September 25.

The Economist. 1992. *Guide to Economic Indicators: Making Sense of Economics.* London: Random Century House.

Edwards, Franklin R. 1997. "The Transformation of the U.S. Financial System: Public Policy Implications." In George M. von Furstenberg (ed.), *The Banking and Financial Structure in the NAFTA Countries and Chile.* Norwell, MA: Kluwer Academic Publishers, Inc.

Edwards, Franklin R. and Frederic S. Mishkin. 1995. "The Decline of Traditional Banking: Implications for Financial Stability and Regulatory Policy." Working Paper No. 4993. National Bureau of Economic Research. January.

Eggertsson, Thráinn. 1990. *Economic Behavior and Institutions.* Cambridge, U.K: Cambridge University Press.

Elliehausen, Gregory. 1998. "The Cost of Bank Regulation: A Review of the Evidence." Staff Study 171. Board of Governors of the Federal Reserve System. Washington, D.C.

Ellis, Joseph J. [1996] 1998. *American Sphinx: The Character of Thomas Jefferson.* New York, NY: Vintage Books.

Evanoff, Douglas and Diana Fortier. 1986. "Geographic Expansion in Commercial Banking: Inferences From Intrastate Activity." In Baer, Herbert and Sue F. Gregorash (eds.), *Toward Nationwide Banking: A Guide To The Issues.* Chicago, IL: Federal Reserve Bank of Chicago.

Federal Deposit Insurance Corporation. 2002. *Historical Statistics On Banking.* Washington, D.C.

_____. 1997. *History of the Eighties – Lessons for the Future: An Examination of the Banking Crises of the 1980s and Early 1990s.* Division of Research and Statistics. December.

Fehr, Ernst and Klaus M. Schmidt. 1998. "A Theory of Fairness, Competition, and Cooperation." Mimeo. July.

Feldman, Ron. 1995. "Will the Securitization Revolution Spread?" *The Region.* The Federal Reserve Bank of Minneapolis. September.

Fiorina, Morris. 1977. *Congress: Keystone of the Washington Establishment.* New Haven, CT: Yale University Press.

Frey, Bruno S. 1997. *Not Just for the Money: An Economic Theory of Personal Motivation.* U.K: Cheltenham. Edward Elgar.

Gilligan, Thomas W., William J. Marshall, and Barry R. Weingast. 1989. "Regulation and the Theory of Legislative Choice: The Interstate Commerce Act of 1887." *Journal of Law and Economics* **XXXII**, April.

Ginsburg, Douglas H. 1981. "Interstate Banking." *Hofstra Law Review Special Issue* **9**(4).

Golden, Claudia and Gary D. Libecap (eds.). 1994. *The Regulated Economy: A Historical Approach to Political Economy.* National Bureau of Economics Research Report. Chicago, IL: University of Chicago Press.

Golembe Associates, Inc. 1979. *A Study of Interstate Banking By Bank Holding Companies.* Prepared for Association of Bank Holding Companies. Washington, D.C.

Gordon, John Steele. 1999. *The Great Game: the Emergence of Wall Street as a World Power, 1653–2000.* New York, NY: Scribner.

Hammond, Bray. 1957. *Banks and Politics in America from the Revolution to the Civil War.* Princeton, NJ: Princeton University Press.

Hammond, Thomas H. and Jack H. Knott. 1988. "The Deregulatory Snowball: Explaining Deregulation in the Financial Industry." *Journal of Politics* **50** (February): 3–30.

Haraf, William S. and Rose Marie Kushmeider (eds.). 1988. *Restructuring Banking and Financial Services in America.* Washington, D.C.: American Enterprise Institute for Public Policy Research.

Hart, Jeffrey. 1992. *Rival Capitalists: International Competitiveness in the U.S., Japan, and Western Europe.* Ithaca, NY: Cornell University Press.

Havrilesky, Thomas. 1989. "Market Failure and Public Choice Theories of Banking Regulation and Deregulation." In George G. Kaufman (ed.), *Research in Financial Services. Vol. 1. Private and Public Policy: A Research Annual.* Greenwich, CT: JAI Press.

Hixson, William F. 1993. *Triumph of the Bankers: Money and Banking the 18th and 19th Centuries.* Westport, CT: Praeger.

Horovitz, Paul M. and Lawrence J. White. 1998. "The Challenges of the New Electronic Technologies in Banking: Private Strategies and Public Policies." Mimeo. November 2. Abstract first published in Social Sciences Research Network Journal: January 18, 1997.

Hughes, Joseph P., William Lang, Loretta J. Mester, and Choon-Geol Moon. 1996. "Efficient Banking Under Interstate Branching." *Journal of Money, Credit, and Banking* **28**(4), November: 1045–1071.

Humphrey David B. and Lawrence B. Pulley. 1997. "Banks' Responses to Deregulation: Profits, Technology, and Efficiency." *Journal of Money, Credit, and Banking* **19**(1), February: 73–93.

Hurst, James Willard. 1982. *Law and Markets in U.S. History.* Madison: University of Wisconsin Press.

Joskow, Paul L. and Nancy L. Rose. 1989. "The Effects of Economic Regulation." In Richard Schmalensee and Robert Willig (eds.), *Handbook of Industrial Organization*, Volume II. Amsterdam, The Netherlands: North Holland.

Kamarck, Andrew. 2001. *Economics for the Twenty-first Century: The Economics of the Economist-Fox.*

Kane, Edward J. 1996. "De Jure Interstate Banking: Why Only Now?" *Journal of Money, Credit, and Banking* **28**(2), May.

_____. 1994. "Financial Reform as a Market-Constrained Political Process." Deakin University Faculty of Management, Working Paper Series No. 9424, September.

_____. 1988. "How Market Forces Influence the Structure of Financial Regulation." In Haraf, William S. and Rose Marie Kushmeider (ed.), *Restructuring Banking and Financial Services in America.* American Enterprise Institute.

_____. 1984. "Deregulation and Change in the Financial Services Industry: Technological and Regulatory Forces in the Developing Fusion of Financial Services Competition." *The Journal of Finance*, **XXXIX**(3), July, 759–773.

_____. 1981. "Impact of Regulation on Economic Behavior: Accelerating Inflation, Technological Innovation, and the Decreasing Effectiveness of Banking Regulation." *The Journal of Finance* **XXXVI**(2), May: 355–367.

Kindleberger, Charles P. 1996 [1978]. *Manias, Panics, and Crashes: A History of Financial Crises.* New York, NY: John Wiley & Sons.

Klein, Peter G. and Marc R. Saidenberg. 1998. "Diversification, Organization, and Efficiency: Evidence from Bank Holding Companies." Working paper.

Klausner, Michael and Lawrence J. White. 1993. *Structural Change in Banking.* Homewood, IL: Business One Irwin.

Kroszner, Randall S. 1998. "Rethinking Bank Regulation: A Review of the Historical Evidence." *Bank of America Journal of Applied Corporate Finance* **11**(2), Summer.

_____. 1997. "The Political Economy of Banking and Financial Regulation in the United States." In George M. von Furstenberg (ed.), *The Banking and Financial Structure in the NAFTA Countries and Chile.* Norwell, MA: Kluwer Academic Publishers, Inc.

Kroszner, Randall S. and Philip E. Strahan. 1998. "What Drives Deregulation? Economics and Politics of the Relaxation of Bank Branching Restrictions." Working Paper 6637. Cambridge, MA: National Bureau of Economic Research.

Laffont, Jean-Jacques, and Jean Tirole. 1993. *A Theory of Incentives in Procurement and Regulation.* Cambridge, MA: MIT Press.

Lawrence, Robert J. 1967. *The Performance of Bank Holding Companies.* Staff Study. Washington, D.C.: Board of Governors of the Federal Reserve System.

Lindblom, Charles. 1979. "Muddling Still Not Through." *Public Administration Review*, November/December.

Light, Jay. 1995. "The Use of Derivatives." In Cathy E. Minehan and Katerina Simons. "Managing Risk in the '90s: What Should You Be Asking about Derivatives?" *New England Economic Review* September/October.

McCubbins, Mathew D., Roger G. Noll, and Barry R. Weingast. 1987. "Administrative Procedures as Instruments of Political Control." *Journal of Law, Economics, and Organization* **3**(2), Fall.

Minehan, Cathy E. and Katerina Simons. 1995. "Managing Risk in the '90s: What Should You Be Asking about Derivatives?" *New England Economic Review*, September/October.

Moe, Terry. 1989. "The Politics of Bureaucratic Structure." In John Chubb and Paul Peterson (eds.), *Can the Government Govern.* Washington, D.C.: The Brookings Institution.

_____. 1984. "The New Economics of Organization." *American Journal of Political Science* **18** (November): 739–777.

Moore, Gordon. 1997. "An Update on Moore's Law." Intel Developer Forum Keynote Address. September 30, 1997. San Francisco, CA: Intel Press Room.

Mowery, David C. 1992. "Finance and Corporate Evolution in Five Industrial Economies, 1900-1950, Industrial and Corporate Change." In Audretsch, David. B. (ed.), *Industrial Policy and Competitive Advantage.* Chapter 22, Volume II. Cheltenham, Glos., U.K.; Northampton, MA: Edward Elgar Publishing.

Musgrave, Richard A. 1959. *The Theory of Public Finance.* New York: McGraw-Hill.

Nelson, Richard R. 1995. "Recent Evolutionary Theorizing About Economic Change." *Journal of Economic Literature* **33**(1): 48–90.

Niskanen, William A. Jr. 1971. *Bureaucracy and Representative Government.* Chicago, IL: Atherton.

Noll, Roger G. 1989a. "Economic Perspectives on the Politics of Regulation." In Richard Schmalensee and Robert Willig (eds.), *Handbook of Industrial Organization*, Volume II. Amsterdam, The Netherlands: North-Holland.

_____. 1989b. "Comment." In Sam Peltzman (ed.), *The Economic Theory of Regulation after a Decade of Deregulation.* Brookings Papers on Economic Activity, Microeconomics.

Noll, Roger G. and B.M. Owen. 1983. *The Political Economy of Deregulation.* Washington, D.C.: American Enterprise Institute.

North, Douglass. 1993. *Institutions, Institutional Change and Economic Performance.* Cambridge: Cambridge University Press.

_____. 1981. *Structure and Change in Economic History.* New York, NY: W.W. Norton & Company.

Olson, Mancur. 1965. *The Logic of Collective Action.* Cambridge, MA: Harvard University Press.

Ostrom, Elinor. 1998. "The Comparative Study of Public Economies." Acceptance Paper for the Frank E. Seidman Distinguished Award in Political Economy. Memphis, TN: P.K. Seidman Foundation. February.

Ostrom, Elinor, Larry Schroeder, and Susan Wynne. 1993. *Institutional Incentives and Sustainable Development: Infrastructure Policies in Perspective.* Boulder, CO.: Westview.

Ostrom, Vincent. 1997. *The Meaning of Democracy and the Vulnerability of Democracies: A Response to Tocqueville's Challenge.* Ann Arbor, MI: University of Michigan Press.

_____. 1994. *The Meaning of American Federalism.* San Francisco, CA: ICS Press.

_____. 1972. "Polycentricity." Workshop in Political Theory and Policy Analysis. Working Paper W72-2.

_____. [1971] 1987. *The Political Theory of a Compound Republic.* Omaha, NB: University of Nebraska Press.

Ostrom, Vincent, Charles M. Tiebout, and Robert Warren. 1961. "The Organization of Government in Metropolitan Areas: A Theoretical Inquiry." *American Political Science Review* **55** (December) 831–842.

Peltzman, Sam. 1989. "The Economic Theory of Regulation after a Decade of Deregulation," Brookings Papers on Economic Activity, Microeconomics.

_____. 1976. "Toward A More General Theory of Regulation," *Journal of Law and Economics.*

Pigou, A.C. 1932. *The Economics of Welfare*, 4th ed. London, U.K.: Macmillan.

Pilloff, Steven J. and Anthony J. Santomero. 1997. "The Value of Effects of Bank Mergers and Acquisitions." Wharton Financial Institutions Working Paper 97-07. The Wharton School. University of Pennsylvania.

Polski, Margaret M. 2001. "Measuring Transaction Costs and Institutional Change in the U.S. Commercial Banking Industry." Institute for Development Studies Discussion Paper 01-3, Indiana University, January.

_____. 1997. "Legislation Games: A Theoretical Framework for Analyzing the Process of Changing Federal Economic Legislation." Prepared for the American Political Science Association Annual Conference.

Polski, Margaret M. and Elinor Ostrom. 1999. "An Institutional Framework for Policy Analysis and Design." Workshop in Political Theory and Policy Analysis Working Paper No. W98-27. June 15.

Porter, Michael E. 1980. *Competitive Strategy; Techniques for Analyzing Industries and Competitors.* New York, NY: Free Press.

Posner, Richard A. 1974. "Theories of Economic Regulation," *Bell Journal of Economics and Management* **5**.

_____. 1971. "Taxation by Regulation." *Bell Journal of Economics and Management* **2**: 22–50.

Rabin, Robert. 1986. "Federal Regulation in Historical Perspective." *Stanford Law Review* **38** (May): 1189–1326.

Redlich, Fritz. 1968. *The Molding of American Banking: Men and Ideas.* New York, NY: Johnson Reprint Corporation.

Richter, Rudolf. 1989/90. "Banking Regulation as Seen by the New Institutional Economics." In Eirik G. Furubotn and Rudolf Richter (eds.), *The Economics and Law of Banking Regulation*, Occasional Papers Vol. 2, Winter, Center for the Study of the New Institutional Economics, Universität des Saarlandes.

Rhoades, Stephen A. 2000. "Bank Mergers and Banking Structure in the U.S. 1980–1998. Staff Study No. 174. Board of Governors of the Federal Reserve. Washington, D.C.

_____. 1994. "A Study of Merger Performance Studies in Banking, 1980–93, and an Assessment of the 'Operating Performance' and 'Event Study' Methodologies." Staff Study No. 167. Board of Governors of the Federal Reserve. Washington, D.C.

Rhoades, Stephen A. and Roger D. Rutz. 1979. "Impact of Bank Holding Companies on Competition and Performance in Banking Markets." Staff Study. Washington, D.C.: Board of Governors of the Federal Reserve.

Romer, Paul. 1994. "The Origins of Endogenous Growth." *Journal of Economic Perspectives* **8**(1): 3–22.

Rose, Peter S. 1997. *Banking Across State Lines: Public and Private Consequences.* Westport, CT: Quorum Books.

Rose, John T. 1978. "Bank Holding Companies As Operational Single Entities." In Board of Governors of the Federal Reserve, *The Bank Holding Company Movement to 1978: A Compendium*. Staff Study. Washington, D.C.

Santomero, Anthony M. 1997. "Deposit Insurance: Do We Need It and Why?" Wharton Financial Institutions Working Paper 97-35. The Wharton School. University of Pennsylvania.

Santomero, Anthony M. and David L. Eckles. 2000. "The Determinants of Success in the New Financial Services Environment: Now That Firms Can Do Everything, What Should They Do and Why Should Regulators Care?" Working Paper 00-32. The Wharton Financial Institutions Center. The Wharton School. University of Pennsylvania.

Sato, Setsuya, John Hawkins, and Aleksander Berentsen. 2001. "E-Finance: Recent Developments and Policy Implications." In BRIE-IGCC E-conomy Project, *Tracking a Transformation: E-Commerce and the Terms of Competition in Industries.* Washington, D.C.: The Brookings Institution Press.

Saunders, Anthony. 1988. "Bank Holding Companies: Structure, Performance, and Reform." In William S. Haraf and Rose Marie Kushmeider (eds.), *Restructuring Banking and Financial Services in America.* Washington, D.C.: American Enterprise Institute for Public Policy Research.

Savage, Donald T. 1978. "A History of the Bank Holding Company Movement, 1900–78." In *The Bank Holding Company Movement to 1978: A Compendium.* Staff Study. Board of Governors of the Federal Reserve. Washington, D.C.

Scherer, F.M. 1999. *New Perspectives on Economic Growth and Technological Innovation.* Washington, D.C.: British-North American Committee, Brookings Institution Press.

Scherer, F. M. and David Ross. 1990. *Industrial Market Structure and Economic Performance.* Boston, MA: Houghton Mifflin Company.

Schleifer, Andrei and Robert W. Vishny. 1998. *The Grabbing Hand: Government Pathologies and Their Cures.* Cambridge, MA: Harvard University Press.

Schumpeter, Joseph A. [1947] 1976. *Capitalism, Socialism, and Democracy.* New York, NY: Harper Torchbooks.

Sen, Amartyz Kumar. 2001. *Development As Freedom.* Oxford; New York: Oxford University Press.

Shepsle, Kenneth A. and Barry R. Weingast. 1994. "Positive Theories of Congressional Institutions." *Legislative Studies Quarterly* **XIX**, 2 May.

Shull, Bernard and Lawrence J. White. "Of Firewalls and Subsidiaries: The Right Stuff for Expanded Bank Activities." New York University Center for Law and Business Working Paper CLB-98-017. February.

Simon, Herbert. 1986. "Rationality in Psychology and Economics." *Journal of Business* **59**(4): pt. 2.

_____. 1982. *Models of Bounded Rationality: Empirically Grounded Economic Reason.* Vol. 3. Cambridge, MA: MIT Press.

_____. 1959. "Theories of Decision-Making in Economics and Behavioral Science." *The Journal of the American Economic Association* **XLIX**(3).

Smith, Adam. 1776. *An Inquiry Into the Nature and Causes of the Wealth of Nations.* London: W. Strahan & T. Cadell.

Solow, Robert M. 1957. "Technical Change and the Aggregate Production Function." *The Review of Economics and Statistics* **39**(3): 312–320.

_____. 1956. "A Contribution to the Theory of Growth." *The Quarterly Journal of Economics* **70**(1): 65–94.

Standard and Poor's. *Banking Industry Survey.* November 20, 1997.

Stigler, George J. 1992. "Law or Economics?" *Journal of Law and Economics* **V. XXXV**, October.

_____. ed. 1988. *Chicago Studies in Political Economy.* Chicago, IL: The University of Chicago Press.

_____. 1971. "The Theory of Economic Regulation." *Bell Journal of Economics and Management* **2**.

Stiglitz, Joseph E. 1989. *The Economic Role of the State.* Oxford, U.K.: Basil Blackwell.

Stokey, Edith and Richard Zeckhauser. 1978. *A Primer for Policy Analysis.* New York, NY: W.W. Norton & Co.

U.S. Census Bureau. 2001. *Statistical Abstract of the United States: 2001.* Washington, D.C.: U.S. Government Printing Office.

U.S. Department of the Treasury. 1991. "Modernizing the Financial System: Recommendations for Safer, More Competitive Banks." February. Washington, D.C.: U.S. Government Printing Office.

U.S. Government. June 22, 1993. "Costs and Benefits of Interstate Banking and Branching: Hearing Before the Subcommittee on Financial Institutions Supervision, Regulation and Deposit Insurance of the Committee on Banking, Finance and Urban Affairs, House of Representatives, 103rd Congress, First Session." Serial No. 103-48. Washington, D.C.: U.S. Government Printing Office.

_____. May 8, 14, 15, 22, June 11, 13, 18, 19, & 20, 1985. "Comprehensive Reform in the Financial Services Industry, Part I & II, Hearings Before the Committee on Banking, Housing, and Urban Affairs, 99th Congress, Senate, First Session." Serial No. 99-120/pt. 1&2. Washington, D.C.: U.S. Government Printing Office.

_____. April 24 & 25, 1985. "Interstate Banking: Hearings Before the Subcommittee on Financial Institutions Supervision, Regulation and Insurance of the Committee on Banking, Finance and Urban Affairs, House of Representatives, 99th Congress, First Session." Serial No. 99-17. Washington,

D.C.: U.S. Government Printing Office.

_____. October 19, 1981. "Financial Institutions Restructuring and Services Act of 1981, Part II: Hearings Before the Committee on Banking, Housing, and Urban Affairs, 97th Congress, Senate, First Session." Serial No. 97-37/pt. 2. Washington, D.C.: U.S. Government Printing Office.

_____. April 18, May 6 & 7, 1981. "Competition and Conditions in the Financial System, Part I: Hearings Before the Committee on Banking, Housing, and Urban Affairs, 97th Congress, Senate, First Session." Serial No. 97-15/pt. 1. Washington, D.C.: U.S. Government Printing Office.

_____. 1981. "Geographic Restrictions on Commercial Banking in the United States." President's Report. January. Washington, D.C.: U.S. Government Printing Office.

_____. 1979. "Hearings on Financial Structure and Regulation Before the Subcommittee on Financial Institutions of the Senate Committee on Banking, Housing, and Urban Affairs, 93rd Congress, Senate, First Session." Washington, D.C.: U.S. Government Printing Office.

Vietor, Richard H.K. 1994. *Contrived Competition: Regulation and Deregulation in America.* Cambridge, MA: Belknap Press.

von Hagen, Jürgen and Ingo Fender. 1998. "Central Bank Policy in a More Perfect Financial System." *Open Economies Review.* The Netherlands: Kluwer Academic Publishers **9**: S1 493–531.

Wallis, John Joseph and Douglass C. North. 1986. "Measuring the Transaction Sector in the American Economy, 1870–1970." In Stanley L. Engerman and Robert E. Gallman (eds.), *Longterm Factors in American Economic Growth*, Vol. 51 of Studies in Income and Wealth series. Chicago, IL: University of Chicago Press.

Wallis, John Joseph, Richard E. Sylla, and John B. Legler. 1994. "The Interaction of Taxation and Regulation in Nineteenth-Century U.S. Banking." In Claudia Golden and Gary Libecap (eds.), *The Regulated Economy: A Historical Approach to Political Economy.* A NBER Project Report. Chicago, IL: University of Chicago Press.

Weingast, Barry R. 1981. "Regulation, Re-regulation, and Deregulation: The Political Foundations of Agency Clientele Relationships." *Journal of Law and Contemporary Problems* **44**(1): 147–177.

Weiss, Leonard W. and Michael W. Klass (eds.), 1986. *Regulatory Reform: What Actually Happened.* Boston, MA: Little, Brown and Company.

_____. 1981. *Case Studies in Regulation.* Boston, MA: Little, Brown.

Weimer, David L. and Aidan R. Vining. 1992. *Policy Analysis: Concepts and Practice.* Englewood Cliffs, N.J.: Prentice-Hall, Inc.

White, Lawrence J. 1986. "The Partial Deregulation of Banks and Other Depository Institutions." In Leonard W. Weiss and Michael W. Klass (eds.), *Regulatory Reform: What Actually Happened.* Boston, MA: Little, Brown and Company.

Wildavsky, Aaron. 1987. *Speaking Truth to Power.* New Brunswick: Transaction Publishers.

Williamson, Oliver E. 1985. *The Economic Institutions of Capitalism.* New York, NY: Free Press.

_____. 1996. *The Mechanisms of Governance.* New York: Oxford University Press.

Wilson, James Q. 1980. *The Politics of Regulation.* New York, NY: Basic Books.

Wilson, Woodrow. [1887] 1956. *Congressional Government: A Study in American Politics.* New York: Meridian Books.

World Bank. 2002. "Building Institutions for Markets." *World Development Report.* International Bank for Reconstruction and Development. World Bank. Washington, D.C.

_____. 2000/2001. "Attacking Poverty." *World Development Report.* International Bank for Reconstruction and Development. World Bank. Washington, D.C.

_____. 1997. "The State in a Changing World." *World Development Report.* International Bank for Reconstruction and Development. World Bank. Washington, D.C.

Yingling, Edward L. 1994. "Interstate Banking: A Lobbyist's Perspective On How It Happened." *Banking Policy Report.* Vol. 13, No. 20. Englewood Cliffs, NJ: Prentice Hall Law and Business.

Zysman, John. 1983. *Governments, Markets, and Growth: Financial Systems and the Politics of Industrial Change.* Ithaca, NY: Cornell University Press.

Appendix 1: Short-Term Interest Rates (3 month Treasury Bill)

Year	Percent	Year	Percent
1960	2.95	1981	14.07
1961	2.38	1982	10.72
1962	2.78	1983	8.62
1963	3.16	1984	9.57
1964	3.55	1985	7.49
1965	3.95	1986	5.97
1966	4.88	1987	5.83
1967	4.33	1988	6.67
1968	5.35	1989	8.11
1969	6.69	1990	7.51
1970	6.44	1991	5.42
1971	4.34	1992	3.45
1972	4.07	1993	3.00
1973	7.02	1994	4.25
1974	7.87	1995	5.49
1975	5.82	1996	5.01
1976	5.00	1997	5.06
1977	5.27	1998	4.78
1978	7.22	1999	4.64
1979	10.04	2000	5.82
1980	11.61		

Source: Board of Governors of the Federal Reserve System. Percent per annum.

Appendix 2: Income of Insured Commercial Banks and Trust Companies

Year	Interest Income	Non-interest Income	Total Income	Annual Change	Net Income	Annual Change	Pre-Tax Net Opr Income	Annual Change	Non-interest Income as % Total Income
1960	9176	1578	10754	11%	2257	45%	3532	13%	15%
1961	9540	1550	11090	3%	2374	5%	3371	–5%	14%
1962	10570	1660	12230	10%	2348	–1%	3406	1%	14%
1963	11770	1750	13520	11%	2393	2%	3502	3%	13%
1964	13111	1950	15061	11%	2602	9%	3764	7%	13%
1965	14715	2114	16829	12%	2861	10%	3891	3%	13%
1966	17136	2381	19517	16%	2857	–0%	4279	10%	12%
1967	19153	2638	21791	12%	3456	21%	4637	8%	12%
1968	22502	2985	25487	17%	3792	10%	5498	19%	12%
1969	27285	3522	30807	21%	4335	14%	6730	22%	11%
1970	30513	4203	34716	13%	4837	12%	7127	6%	12%
1971	31618	4746	36364	5%	5236	8%	6713	–6%	13%
1972	35014	5233	40247	11%	5654	8%	7250	8%	13%
1973	47037	6000	53037	32%	6580	16%	8706	20%	11%
1974	61233	6928	68161	29%	7092	8%	9251	6%	10%
1975	57917	8643	66560	–2%	7257	2%	8979	–3%	13%
1976	73033	7631	80664	21%	7844	8%	9915	10%	9%
1977	82252	8106	90358	12%	8881	13%	11567	17%	9%
1978	103957	9624	113581	26%	10758	21%	15100	31%	8%
1979	138900	11382	150282	32%	12839	19%	17892	18%	8%
1980	176422	14349	190771	27%	14010	9%	19505	9%	8%
1981	231286	17520	248806	30%	14722	5%	20132	3%	7%
1982	238344	20184	258528	4%	14844	1%	19034	–5%	8%
1983	217225	23269	240494	–7%	14931	1%	18895	–1%	10%
1984	250353	26512	276865	15%	15502	4%	20146	7%	10%
1985	248220	31054	279274	1%	17977	16%	21813	8%	11%
1986	237766	35877	273643	–2%	17419	–3%	18457	–15%	13%
1987	244840	41481	286321	5%	2803	–84%	6580	–64%	14%
1988	272277	44953	317230	11%	24812	785%	33709	412%	14%
1989	317371	50916	368287	16%	15575	–37%	24004	–29%	14%
1990	320476	54899	375375	2%	15991	3%	22567	–6%	15%

Appendix 2 (Continued)

Year	Interest Income	Non-interest Income	Total Income	Annual Change	Net Income	Annual Change	Pre-Tax Net Opr Income	Annual Change	Non-interest Income as % Total Income
1991	289214	59739	348953	–7%	17935	12%	22542	–0%	17%
1992	255223	65648	320871	–8%	31987	78%	42053	87%	20%
1993	245055	74954	320009	–0%	43035	35%	57758	37%	23%
1994	257828	76276	334104	4%	44622	4%	67627	17%	23%
1995	302383	82426	384809	15%	48745	9%	74304	10%	21%
1996	312742	162754	475496	24%	52350	7%	79339	7%	34%
1997	339541	104499	444040	–7%	59156	13%	89166	12%	24%
1998	362019	123699	485718	9%	61785	4%	90094	1%	25%
1999	367322	144400	511722	5%	71556	16%	110583	23%	28%
2000	427985	152751	580736	13%	71176	–1%	111534	1%	26%

Source: Author's estimates based on FDIC (2000).
Calendar year basis in millions of dollars.

Appendix 3: Financial Performance of Insured Commercial Banks and Trust Companies

Year	Interest Income	Interest Expense	Non-interest Income	Non-interest Expense	Pre-Tax Net Opr Income	Total Assets	Cash & Due From
1960	9176	1874	1578	5142	3532	256322	51902
1961	9540	2146	1550	5383	3371	277374	56181
1962	10570	2911	1660	5746	3406	295983	53799
1963	11770	3574	1750	6206	3502	311790	50445
1964	13111	4241	1950	6780	3764	345130	60033
1965	14715	5316	2114	7298	3891	375394	60437
1966	17136	6629	2381	8192	4279	402946	68652
1967	19153	7730	2638	8977	4637	450713	77533
1968	22502	9311	2985	10255	5498	500238	83270
1969	27285	11530	3522	12026	6730	524665	89355
1970	30513	12454	4203	14432	7127	570167	93048
1971	31618	13595	4746	15189	6713	633573	98691
1972	35014	15602	5233	16422	7250	730903	111844
1973	47037	24492	6000	18574	8706	820515	116940
1974	61233	35075	6928	21549	9251	1037338	178295
1975	57917	30240	8643	23729	8979	1086409	189407
1976	73033	39328	7631	27730	9915	1182390	203772
1977	82252	44565	8106	30925	11567	1339392	242983
1978	103957	59383	9624	35573	15100	1508331	274076
1979	138900	87912	11382	40692	17892	1692080	306602
1980	176422	120123	14349	46664	19505	1855695	331936
1981	231286	169857	17520	53686	20132	2029151	327481
1982	238344	169372	20184	61615	19034	2193867	334299
1983	217225	143887	23269	66910	18895	2341955	341793
1984	250353	169084	26512	73818	20146	2508871	323727
1985	248220	157323	31054	82365	21813	2730672	340689
1986	237766	142829	35877	90250	18457	2940699	379331
1987	244840	144953	41481	97244	6580	2999949	358339
1988	272277	165028	44953	101329	33709	3130796	355563
1989	317371	205142	50916	108121	24004	3299362	350234
1990	320476	204952	54899	115768	22567	3389490	318016
1991	289214	167302	59739	124795	22542	3430682	304862
1992	255223	121805	65648	130965	42053	3505663	298077
1993	245055	105742	74954	139695	57758	3706165	272961
1994	257828	111278	76276	144234	67627	4010517	303546
1995	302383	148173	82426	149728	74304	4312676	306522
1996	312742	149989	162754	160698	79339	4578314	335988
1997	339541	165038	104499	169983	89166	5014942	355107
1998	362019	179266	123699	194143	90094	5442588	356704
1999	367322	175129	144400	204196	110583	5734761	366455
2000	427985	224195	152751	215753	111534	6238713	369811

Appendix 3 (Continued)

Year	Fixed Assets	Other Assets	Earning Assets	Equity	ROTA	NIM	Capital Ratio
1960	2829	2674	198917	20635	1.38%	3.67%	8.05%
1961	3102	3180	214911	22101	1.22%	3.44%	7.97%
1962	3403	3364	235417	23732	1.15%	3.25%	8.02%
1963	3945	3545	253855	25193	1.12%	3.23%	8.08%
1964	4754	4288	276055	26627	1.09%	3.21%	7.72%
1965	5144	5048	304765	28252	1.04%	3.08%	7.53%
1966	5620	5933	322741	29963	1.06%	3.26%	7.44%
1967	6007	6917	360256	32022	1.03%	3.17%	7.10%
1968	6657	8764	401547	34518	1.10%	3.29%	6.90%
1969	8070	11100	416140	37687	1.28%	3.79%	7.18%
1970	9143	12392	455584	40590	1.25%	3.96%	7.12%
1971	10285	13500	511097	44062	1.06%	3.53%	6.95%
1972	11525	15664	591870	48387	0.99%	3.28%	6.62%
1973	12789	17994	672792	54957	1.06%	3.35%	6.70%
1974	14675	32279	812089	59221	0.89%	3.22%	5.71%
1975	16054	29362	851586	63854	0.83%	3.25%	5.88%
1976	17243	31474	929901	72248	0.84%	3.62%	6.11%
1977	19010	37065	1040334	79280	0.86%	3.62%	5.92%
1978	21346	52008	1160901	87418	1.00%	3.84%	5.80%
1979	23550	68969	1292959	97242	1.06%	3.94%	5.75%
1980	26654	83741	1413364	107599	1.05%	3.98%	5.80%
1981	30397	105270	1566003	118241	0.99%	3.92%	5.83%
1982	34028	120105	1705435	128698	0.87%	4.04%	5.87%
1983	36637	120672	1842853	140459	0.81%	3.98%	6.00%
1984	38444	123752	2022948	154103	0.80%	4.02%	6.14%
1985	40662	118597	2230724	169118	0.80%	4.07%	6.19%
1986	42663	110646	2408059	182144	0.63%	3.94%	6.19%
1987	44950	117694	2478966	180651	0.22%	4.03%	6.02%
1988	45733	128047	2601453	196546	1.08%	4.12%	6.28%
1989	48212	128718	2772198	204823	0.73%	4.05%	6.21%
1990	51437	133923	2886114	218623	0.67%	4.00%	6.45%
1991	52249	128921	2944650	231711	0.66%	4.14%	6.75%
1992	53103	123149	3031334	263560	1.20%	4.40%	7.52%
1993	55527	136158	3241519	296491	1.56%	4.30%	8.00%
1994	58922	141712	3506337	312084	1.69%	4.18%	7.78%
1995	61425	148850	3795879	349571	1.72%	4.06%	8.11%
1996	64611	164307	4013408	375269	1.73%	4.06%	8.20%
1997	67180	180026	4412629	417773	1.78%	3.95%	8.33%
1998	71308	205815	4808761	462150	1.66%	3.80%	8.49%
1999	73739	231013	5063554	479722	1.93%	3.80%	8.37%
2000	75701	273130	5520071	529583	1.79%	3.69%	8.49%
Average					1.11%	3.75%	6.96%

Source: Author's estimates based on FDIC (2000).
Calendar year basis in millions of dollars.

Appendix 4: Federal Banking Legislation 1863–2000

Year	Legislation
1863	National Currency Act
1864	National Bank Act
1913	Federal Reserve Act
1927	To Amend the National Banking Laws and the Federal Reserve Act (McFadden)
1932	Federal Home Loan Bank Act
1933	Banking Act (Glass-Steagall)
1933	Home Owners' Loan Act
1934	National Housing Act
1934	Federal Credit Union Act
1935	Banking Act
1950	Federal Deposit Insurance Corporation Act
1956	Bank Holding Company Act, including Douglas Amendment
1966	Interest Rate Control Act
1970	Bank Holding Company Act Amendments
1977	Community Reinvestment Act
1978	International Banking Act
1978	Financial Institutions Regulatory and Interest Rate Control Act
1980	Depository Institutions Deregulation and Monetary Control Act
1982	Depository Institutions Act (Garn-St. Germain)
1987	Competitive Equality Banking Act
1989	Financial Institutions Reform, Recovery, and Enforcement Act
1990	Crime Control Act
1991	Federal Deposit Insurance Corporation Improvement Act
1992	Housing and Community Development Act
1994	RTC Completion Act
1994	Community Development and Regulatory Improvement Act
1994	Interstate Banking and Branching Efficiency Act (Reigle-Neal)
1999	Financial Services Modernization Act (Gramm-Leach-Bliley)

Source: Author's compilation based on FDIC statistics and White (1986)